HEART HEALTHY COOKBOOK FOR BEGINNERS

1900+ days of Delicious Low-Sodium and Low-Fat Simple Recipes

for Reducing Cholesterol and Blood Pressure,

Plus an Easy-to-Follow 49-Day Meal Plan

Genny Green

Dear Reader,

Welcome to *Heart-Healthy Cookbook for Beginners*! Eating well doesn't have to be complicated or expensive—heart-healthy meals can be simple, delicious, and budget-friendly. Whether you're looking to improve your heart health, lower cholesterol, or just enjoy wholesome meals, this book is designed to make healthy eating easy and affordable. Each recipe includes clear instructions, nutritious ingredients, and essential nutritional information to help you make informed choices.

I encourage you to have fun in the kitchen, explore new flavors, and embrace the joy of cooking meals that fuel your body and heart. Healthy eating is about balance, variety, and enjoying the process. Thank you for allowing me to be part of your journey—I hope these recipes bring warmth, nourishment, and happiness to your table!

With love and good health,
Genny Green

TABLE OF CONTENTS

UNDERSTANDING HEART HEALTH

Maintaining a healthy heart is crucial for well-being. A diet low in sodium, added sugars, and saturated fats, and rich in heart-supporting nutrients, can reduce the risk of cardiovascular diseases like heart attacks and strokes.

KEY NUTRIENTS FOR HEART HEALTH

1. **Fiber**: Helps lower cholesterol levels and supports healthy digestion. Found in whole grains, fruits, vegetables, and legumes.
2. **Omega-3 Fatty Acids**: Reduce inflammation and lower the risk of heart disease. Present in fatty fish (such as mackerel and salmon), walnuts, and flaxseeds.
3. **Antioxidants**: Protect the heart by reducing oxidative stress. Found in berries, dark chocolate, and green leafy vegetables.
4. **Potassium**: Helps regulate blood pressure. Found in bananas, oranges, potatoes, and spinach.
5. **Magnesium**: Supports heart muscle function. Present in seeds, nuts, whole grains, as well as in leafy green vegetables.

HEART-HEALTHY COOKING TECHNIQUES

1. **Grilling and Baking**: Use these methods instead of frying to reduce the intake of unhealthy fats.
2. **Steaming and Poaching**: Preserve the nutrients in vegetables and fish without adding extra fats.
3. **Using Healthy Fats**: Opt for olive oil or avocado oil instead of butter or margarine.
4. **Reducing Sodium**: Use herbs, spices, and lemon juice to flavor food instead of salt.

BUILDING A HEART-HEALTHY PLATE

1. **Fill Half Your Plate with Vegetables and Fruits**: Aim for a variety of colors to ensure a range of nutrients.
2. **Choose Whole Grains**: Opt for whole-grain bread, brown rice, quinoa, and oats.
3. **Include Lean Proteins**: Choose fish, poultry, beans, and legumes. Limit red meat and processed meats.
4. **Incorporate Healthy Fats**: Add nuts, seeds, and avocados to your meals.

TIPS FOR A HEART-HEALTHY LIFESTYLE

1. **Switch to a Heart-Healthy Diet:** Diets high in saturated fats, trans fats, added sugars, and sodium can contribute to obesity, high cholesterol, and hypertension.

2. **Control Your Blood Pressure:** High blood pressure (Hypertension) strains the heart and damages blood vessels, increasing the risk of heart disease.

3. **Control Your Weight:** Excess body weight increases the strain on the heart and is closely linked to hypertension, diabetes, and high cholesterol.

4. **Stay Active**: Aim for at least 30 minutes of moderate exercise most days of the week.

5. **Stay well-hydrated:** Drink at least 8–10 glasses of water daily to maintain proper hydration.

6. **Manage Stress**: Practice relaxation techniques such as yoga, meditation, or deep breathing.

7. **Avoid Smoking**: Smoking is a major risk factor for heart disease.

8. **Avoid excessive alcohol consumption:** Drinking too much alcohol can lead to high blood pressure, irregular heart rhythms, and cardiomyopathy.

By incorporating these heart-healthy basics into your daily routine, you can take proactive steps toward maintaining a healthy heart and overall well-being. Enjoy experimenting with delicious and nutritious recipes that support your heart health.

DEBUNKING MYTHS ABOUT HEART-HEALTHY EATING

There are many misconceptions about what constitutes a heart-healthy diet. Understanding and debunking these myths can help you make informed decisions for your cardiovascular health. Here's the truth behind common myths:

Myth 1: You Should Avoid All Fats

- **Truth:** Not all fats are bad. Healthy fats, such as unsaturated fats found in avocados, nuts, seeds, and olive oil, are essential for heart health. They help reduce LDL (bad) cholesterol and increase HDL (good) cholesterol. It's the trans fats and excessive saturated fats that should be minimized.

Myth 2: A Heart-Healthy Diet is Bland and Restrictive

- **Truth:** Heart-healthy eating is about balance and variety, not deprivation. You can enjoy a wide range of flavorful foods, including spices, herbs, fruits, vegetables, lean proteins, and whole grains. Even occasional indulgences are okay if you maintain overall healthy habits.

Myth 3: Carbs Are Bad for Your Heart

- **Truth:** Not all carbohydrates are harmful. Refined carbs like white bread and sugary snacks can increase blood sugar and the risk of heart disease. However, whole grains like quinoa, oats, and brown rice are rich in fiber and beneficial for heart health.

Myth 4: All Salt is Bad

- **Truth:** While excessive sodium can raise blood pressure, not all salt needs to be avoided entirely. The key is moderation and choosing low-sodium options. Potassium-rich foods like bananas, sweet potatoes, and spinach help counterbalance sodium's effects.

Myth 5: Only Red Meat is Bad

- **Truth:** While red meat can be high in saturated fats, lean cuts, and moderate portions can fit into a heart-healthy diet. It's also essential to focus on plant-based proteins, fish, and poultry to diversify protein sources.

Myth 6: Heart-Healthy Eating is Expensive

- **Truth:** Eating heart-healthy can be affordable with some planning. Whole foods like beans, lentils, oats, frozen vegetables, and canned low-sodium fish are cost-effective and nutritious. Preparing meals at home can save money compared to dining out.

Myth 7: You Have to Cut Out All Sugar

- **Truth:** While it's essential to limit added sugars, naturally occurring sugars in fruits, dairy, and whole foods are part of a balanced diet. Focus on reducing processed foods and sugary drinks while enjoying natural sweetness.

Myth 8: Cholesterol in Food is the Main Concern

- **Truth:** Recent research suggests dietary cholesterol (like in eggs) has less impact on blood cholesterol than previously thought. The focus should be on reducing saturated and trans fats, which have a more significant effect on raising LDL cholesterol.

Myth 9: Supplements Can Replace a Heart-Healthy Diet

- **Truth:** While some supplements may support heart health, they cannot replace the benefits of a balanced diet. Whole foods provide fiber, antioxidants, and other nutrients that work together to protect your heart.

Myth 10: Eating Healthy Requires Drastic Changes

- **Truth:** Small, gradual changes to your diet can have a big impact on heart health. Start by swapping refined grains for whole grains, adding more vegetables to meals, and cooking with heart-healthy oils.

KEY TAKEAWAY:

Heart-healthy eating doesn't have to be complicated or restrictive. It's about making informed choices, focusing on whole foods, and maintaining balance and variety in your meals. By understanding and debunking these myths, you can build a sustainable and enjoyable diet that supports your cardiovascular health.

THE IMPACT OF ADDED SUGARS ON HEART HEALTH

Added sugars are harmful to heart health because they contribute to a range of conditions that increase the risk of cardiovascular disease. Here's how added sugars impact the heart:

1. Promote Weight Gain and Obesity

- Foods and beverages high in added sugars are often calorie-dense but lack nutrients, leading to excessive calorie consumption.

- Obesity is a major risk factor for heart disease, as it puts extra strain on the heart and is associated with high blood pressure, high cholesterol, and diabetes.

2. Increase Risk of Type 2 Diabetes

- Diets high in added sugars can cause insulin resistance, a condition where cells don't respond well to insulin, leading to elevated blood sugar levels.

- Type 2 diabetes significantly increases the risk of heart disease and stroke by damaging blood vessels and nerves that control the heart.

3. Elevate Blood Pressure

- Consuming large amounts of sugar, particularly from sugary beverages, has been linked to higher blood pressure levels, which is a key contributor to heart disease.

4. Raise Levels of Triglycerides

- Added sugars, especially fructose, can lead to increased production of triglycerides in the liver. High triglyceride levels in the blood are associated with an increased risk of atherosclerosis (plaque buildup in arteries) and heart attacks.

5. Contribute to Chronic Inflammation

- A diet high in added sugars can trigger low-grade chronic inflammation in the body, which damages blood vessels and contributes to the development of atherosclerosis and heart disease.

6. Reduce HDL (Good) Cholesterol

- High sugar consumption is associated with lower levels of HDL cholesterol, which helps remove LDL (bad cholesterol) from the bloodstream. Lower HDL levels can increase the risk of cardiovascular issues.

RECOMMENDATIONS TO REDUCE ADDED SUGAR INTAKE

- Avoid sugary drinks like sodas, energy drinks, and sweetened teas; opt for water, herbal teas, or unsweetened beverages instead.

- Limit consumption of sweets, baked goods, and desserts, and choose fruit to satisfy sweet cravings.

- Read food labels to identify hidden sugars in processed foods, such as cereals, granola bars, and sauces.

- Aim to keep added sugar intake below 10% of daily calories, as recommended by the American Heart Association.

Reducing added sugar intake can significantly lower the risk of heart disease by improving blood pressure, cholesterol levels, and overall cardiovascular health.

HEART-HEALTHY SWEETENERS FOR BAKERY, DESSERTS, SMOOTHIES, AND BEVERAGES

Here's a categorized list of natural, heart-healthy sweeteners ideal for various culinary applications:

1. **Honey (Raw)**

   - **Benefits**: Antioxidants and natural anti-inflammatory properties.

   - **Use**: Adds moisture to baked goods; reduce liquid in the recipe when substituting for sugar.

2. **Maple Syrup (Pure)**

   - **Benefits**: Contains trace minerals like manganese and zinc.

   - **Use**: Perfect for muffins, cakes, and breads; substitute 3/4 cup maple syrup for every 1 cup sugar.

3. **Coconut Sugar**

- **Benefits**: Low glycemic index; minimally processed.

- **Use**: A 1:1 replacement for granulated sugar in cookies, cakes, and breads.

4. **Date Sugar**

- **Benefits**: Made from dried, ground dates; rich in fiber.

- **Use**: Ideal for dense baked goods like brownies or banana bread.

5. **Applesauce (Unsweetened)**

- **Benefits**: Natural sugars with added moisture and fiber.

- **Use**: Replace up to half the sugar in cakes or muffins; also works as a fat substitute.

DESSERTS (PUDDINGS, ICE CREAMS, CUSTARDS)

6. **Stevia (Liquid or Powder)**

- **Benefits**: Zero-calorie plant-based sweetener.

- **Use**: Works well in custards, puddings, or no-bake desserts; use sparingly as it's very sweet.

7. **Monk Fruit Sweetener**

- **Benefits**: Zero-calorie sweetener with natural antioxidants.

- **Use**: Excellent for ice creams and creamy desserts.

8. **Banana (Mashed or Puréed)**

- **Benefits**: High in potassium and natural sweetness.

- **Use**: Perfect for mousses, custards, or no-bake treats.

9. **Date Syrup**

- **Benefits**: Made from pure dates; retains minerals like potassium.

- **Use**: Drizzle on frozen yogurt or mix into dessert sauces.

10. **Molasses**

- **Benefits**: High in iron, calcium, and potassium.

- **Use**: Best for dark desserts like gingerbread or chocolate puddings.

SMOOTHIES

11. **Dates (Whole or Puréed)**

   - **Benefits**: Fiber-rich and naturally sweet; rich in potassium, magnesium, and fiber.

   - **Use**: Blend with smoothies for creamy sweetness.

12. **Date Syrup**

   - **Benefits**: Made from pure dates; rich in potassium and magnesium.

   - **Use**: Adds natural sweetness to smoothies with just 1–2 teaspoons; pairs well with almond milk, cacao, or berries.

12. **Maple Syrup**

   - **Benefits**: Adds natural sweetness with a hint of caramel flavor.

   - **Use**: Perfect for green smoothies or protein shakes.

13. **Honey**

   - **Benefits**: Soothes the throat and provides quick energy.

   - **Use**: Ideal for fruit-based smoothies.

14. **Banana (Frozen or Fresh)**

   - **Benefits**: Naturally creamy and sweet, high in potassium.

   - **Use**: Blend as a base for almost any smoothie.

15. **Coconut Water**

   - **Benefits**: Hydrating with a hint of natural sweetness.

   - **Use**: Replace milk or water in smoothies for a light, sweet touch.

BEVERAGES (COFFEE, TEA, LEMONADE, COCKTAILS)

16. **Stevia**

    - **Benefits**: Zero-calorie and heat-stable.

    - **Use**: Dissolves well in hot and cold beverages.

17. **Monk Fruit Sweetener**

    - **Benefits**: No impact on blood sugar.

    - **Use**: Great for iced tea, lemonade, or coffee.

18. **Honey**

    - **Benefits**: Adds floral sweetness and soothes the throat.

    - **Use**: Stir into warm beverages like tea or lattes.

19. **Agave Syrup (in Moderation)**

    - **Benefits**: Low glycemic index.

    - **Use**: Mixes easily into cocktails or cold drinks.

20. **Cinnamon or Vanilla**

    - **Benefits**: Adds natural sweetness and warmth without calories.

    - **Use**: Sprinkle or stir into coffee, tea, or hot chocolate.

QUICK TIPS FOR USING SWEETENERS

- **Balance Flavor**: Some natural sweeteners (like molasses) have strong flavors; pair them with complementary ingredients.

- **Adjust Liquid Content**: Liquid sweeteners like honey or maple syrup may require reducing other liquids in your recipe.

- **Experiment with Blends**: Combining sweeteners (e.g., honey and stevia) can balance sweetness and enhance texture.

- **Start Small**: Natural sweeteners can be more potent than sugar; begin with a smaller amount and adjust to taste.

HOW TO REDUCE SATURATED AND TRANS FATS IN YOUR DIET?

Saturated and trans fats pose significant dangers to heart health. Consuming high amounts of saturated fats can raise LDL (low-density lipoprotein) cholesterol levels in the blood, leading to the buildup of plaque in the arteries, a condition known as atherosclerosis. This buildup narrows the arteries, making it harder for blood to flow and increasing the risk of heart attacks and strokes. Additionally, diets high in saturated fats can contribute to obesity, which is a significant risk factor for heart disease.

Trans fats, often found in processed and fried foods, are even more harmful as they not only raise LDL cholesterol but also lower HDL (high-density lipoprotein) cholesterol, further increasing the risk of cardiovascular diseases. Reducing the intake of these unhealthy fats and opting for healthier alternatives can significantly improve heart health and reduce the risk of cardiovascular issues.

HEART-HEALTHY SUBSTITUTES FOR SATURATED AND TRANS FATS

Here are some common products that are high in saturated fats:

1. **Butter**: Replace with ghee used in moderation.

2. **Cheese**: Opt for low-fat or reduced-fat cheese varieties.

3. **Red Meat**: Choose lean cuts of meat such as sirloin, tenderloin, or lean ground beef.

4. **Processed Meats**: Replace processed meats with lean protein sources like grilled chicken, turkey, or fish. Plant-based alternatives like tempeh or seitan can also be great options.

5. **Full-Fat Dairy Products**: Switch to low-fat or fat-free dairy products, such as skim milk, low-fat yogurt, and reduced-fat cheese. Plant-based milk alternatives like almond milk or soy milk can also be used.

6. **Baked Goods**: Use heart-healthy oils like olive oil, grapeseed oil, or ghee instead of butter or shortening.

7. **Fried Foods**: Opt for baking, grilling, or air-frying instead of deep-frying. These methods reduce the amount of added fat while still providing a crispy texture.

WHY IS SODIUM HARMFUL FOR HEART HEALTH?

Sodium can be harmful to the heart primarily because of its effect on blood pressure. Here's a clear explanation of why limiting sodium intake is important for heart health:

1. Sodium and High Blood Pressure

- Sodium causes the body to retain water. When you consume excess sodium, your body holds onto more fluid to dilute the sodium in your bloodstream.

- This increased fluid volume puts extra pressure on your blood vessels, leading to higher blood pressure (hypertension).

- High blood pressure forces your heart to work harder to pump blood, which can strain the heart muscle and damage blood vessels over time.

2. Impact on Heart Health

- High blood pressure is a major risk factor for heart disease, including heart attacks and strokes.

- Over time, elevated blood pressure can lead to thickening and stiffening of the arteries (atherosclerosis), making it harder for blood to flow efficiently.

- This increases the risk of coronary artery disease and heart failure.

3. Sodium and Fluid Balance

- Your kidneys help regulate sodium levels in your body. When you consume too much sodium, it can overwhelm your kidneys' ability to remove it, leading to fluid retention.

- Excess fluid increases blood volume and pressure, putting additional strain on your cardiovascular system.

4. Exacerbation of Other Conditions

- For individuals with conditions like heart failure, kidney disease, or diabetes, managing sodium intake is even more critical, as their bodies are less efficient at handling excess sodium.

- High sodium intake can worsen symptoms such as swelling (edema) and shortness of breath in these conditions.

KEY TAKEAWAYS FOR SODIUM INTAKE

- Limit sodium intake to less than 2,300 mg per day (about one teaspoon of salt) or, ideally, aim for 1,500 mg per day, especially if you are at risk for high blood pressure (according to American Heart Association).

- Be mindful of hidden sodium in processed foods like canned soups, frozen meals, and snacks.

- Use herbs, spices, citrus, and vinegar to flavor foods instead of salt.

SODIUM-RICH INGREDIENTS TO WATCH OUT FOR

Here are some sodium-rich ingredients:

- **Table Salt**: Commonly used in cooking and seasoning, table salt is a primary source of sodium.

- **Soy Sauce**: A popular condiment in many cuisines, soy sauce is high in sodium.

- **Processed Meats**: Items like ham, bacon, and sausages often contain high levels of sodium due to the curing process.

- **Canned products**: Many canned soups, vegetables, meats, fish, and beans have added sodium for flavor and preservation.

- **Cheese**: Certain types of cheese, such as processed cheese and feta, can be high in sodium.

- **Pickles and Olives**: These are often preserved in brine, which is high in sodium.

- **Instant Pudding Mix**: Contains sodium-rich additives for thickening.

- **Baking Soda and Baking Powder**: Contains a considerable amount of sodium.

It's important to be mindful of these ingredients if you're aiming to reduce sodium intake for heart health.

NATURAL HEART-HEALTHY SALT SUBSTITUTES

Here's a list of natural heart-healthy salt substitutes that are free from artificial additives and focus on enhancing flavor while promoting cardiovascular health:

HERBS (FRESH OR DRIED)

1. **Basil**

   - Sweet and slightly peppery.

   - Great for Italian dishes, soups, and roasted vegetables.

2. **Parsley**

   - Fresh and grassy flavor.

   - Perfect for salads, soups, and as a garnish.

3. **Cilantro**

   - Bright and citrusy.

   - Ideal for Mexican, Indian, and Thai dishes.

4. **Oregano**

   - Earthy and slightly bitter.

   - Complements tomato-based sauces, roasted vegetables, and Mediterranean recipes.

5. **Thyme**

   - Woodsy and aromatic.

   - Great for poultry, fish, and roasted root vegetables.

6. **Rosemary**

   - Pine-like and robust.

   - Perfect for potatoes, bread, and grilled meats.

7. **Dill**

  - Fresh and slightly tangy.

  - Great for fish, yogurt sauces, and pickled dishes.

8. **Celery (fresh or seeds)**

  - Naturally salty and aromatic.

  - Use fresh celery or celery seeds in soups and salads.

9. **Sage**

  - Savory and slightly peppery.

  - Ideal for stuffing, poultry, and squash recipes.

SPICES

9. **Garlic Powder or Fresh Garlic**

  - Adds a deep, savory flavor.

  - Works in almost any savory dish.

10. **Onion Powder or Fresh Onion**

  - Sweet and savory depth.

  - Great for soups, casseroles, and spice rubs.

11. **Black Pepper**

  - Enhances natural flavors without adding sodium.

  - Use universally across dishes.

12. **Cumin**

  - Warm and earthy.

  - Ideal for Mexican, Indian, and Middle Eastern dishes.

13. Smoked Paprika

- Sweet, smoky flavor.

- Perfect for roasted vegetables, meats, and stews.

14. Turmeric

- Warm and slightly bitter.

- Excellent for curries, soups, and rice dishes.

15. Ginger (Fresh or Ground)

- Zesty and slightly spicy.

- Great for stir-fries, soups, and marinades.

16. Cayenne Pepper or Chili Flakes

- Adds heat and complexity.

- Ideal for soups, stews, and spice blends.

ACIDIC INGREDIENTS

17. Lemon Juice or Zest

- Bright and tangy.

- Perfect for fish, chicken, vegetables, and dressings.

18. Lime Juice or Zest

- Sharp and citrusy.

- Works well in Mexican, Thai, and seafood dishes.

19. Vinegars

- **Balsamic, Apple Cider, Red Wine, Rice Vinegar**

- Adds a tangy and complex flavor to salads, sauces, and marinades.

20. **Nutritional Yeast**

- Cheesy, nutty flavor.

- Use in soups, sauces, or sprinkle on popcorn.

21. **Seaweed (Nori, Wakame, Dulse)**

- Briny and oceanic.

- Perfect for soups, rice dishes, and salads.

22. **Tomato Paste or Purée**

- Rich and savory with natural sweetness.

- Great for sauces, stews, and soups.

23. **Mushrooms (Fresh or Dried)**

- Deep umami flavor, especially shiitake.

- Ideal for soups, risottos, and sautés.

When substituting fresh herbs for dried herbs in recipes, the general rule of thumb is to use three times the amount of fresh herbs as you would dried herbs. This is because dried herbs have a more concentrated flavor due to the removal of moisture. Here are some common conversions:

- **1 tablespoon of fresh herbs** = **1 teaspoon of dried herbs**

- **3 tablespoons of fresh herbs** = **1 tablespoon of dried herbs**

TIPS FOR USING NATURAL SUBSTITUTES:

- **Combine Flavors**: Layer herbs, spices, and acids for a balanced taste.

- **Experiment**: Try small quantities of new substitutes to find what works best for your dish.

Use Fresh When Possible: Fresh ingredients often have more vibrant flavors than dried.

OVERNIGHT OATS WITH BERRIES

INGREDIENTS

- 1 cup rolled oats
- 1 cup unsweetened almond milk
- 1 cup mixed berries (fresh or frozen)
- 2 tbsp chia seeds
- 1 tsp honey (optional)
- 1/4 tsp vanilla extract (optional)

Serves: 2   **Prep time**: 5 min   **Setting time**: 8 hours (overnight)

DIRECTIONS

Combine oats, almond milk, chia seeds, and optional vanilla in a jar or container overnight.

In the morning, stir the oats again, serve in two bowls and top with mixed berries and honey if desired.

NUTRITIONAL INFORMATION (PER SERVING)

200 calories, 6g protein, 35g carbohydrates, 6g fats, 10g fiber, 0mg cholesterol, 50mg sodium, 70mg magnesium, 200mg potassium.

WHOLE GRAIN BREAD TOAST WITH GUACAMOLE

INGREDIENTS

- 2 slices of whole-grain bread
- 1 ripe avocado, mashed
- 1 tsp lime juice
- 1/4 tsp garlic powder
- 1/4 tsp black pepper
- 1 tbsp chopped fresh cilantro (optional)
- 2–3 cherry tomatoes, halved (optional, for topping)

Serves: 2   **Prep time**: 5 min   **Cook time**: 2 min

DIRECTIONS

Toast whole-grain bread until golden and crisp.

Mash avocado with lemon/lime juice, garlic powder, black pepper, and optional cilantro.

Spread guacamole on toast, top with diced cherry tomatoes (optional), and serve immediately.

NUTRITIONAL INFORMATION (PER SERVING - 1 TOAST)

190 calories, 5g protein, 22g carbohydrates, 11g fats, 7g fiber, 0mg cholesterol, 20mg sodium, 45mg magnesium, 350mg potassium.

GREEK YOGURT PARFAIT WITH GRANOLA AND NUTS

INGREDIENTS

- 1 cup unsweetened Greek yogurt (2% or nonfat)
- 1/2 cup granola (low-sugar or homemade)
- 1/4 cup mixed nuts (e.g., almonds, walnuts, and pecans), chopped
- 1 cup fresh mixed berries (e.g., blueberries, raspberries, strawberries)
- 1 tbsp honey or maple syrup (optional)
- 1 tbsp chia seeds (optional, for added fiber and omega-3s)

Serves: 2   **Prep time**: 5 min

DIRECTIONS

Chop nuts if needed, wash and dry berries.

In two glasses, layer 1/4 cup Greek yogurt. Add 2 tbsp granola, 1 tbsp nuts, and 1/4 cup berries.

Repeat layers. Drizzle honey or maple syrup and sprinkle chia seeds if desired.

NUTRITIONAL INFORMATION (PER SERVING)

290 calories, 12g protein, 33g carbohydrates, 10g fats, 5g fiber, 5mg cholesterol, 80mg sodium, 50mg magnesium, 300mg potassium.

SPINACH AND FETA OMELETTE

INGREDIENTS

- 4 large eggs
- 1 cup fresh spinach, chopped
- 1/4 cup feta cheese, crumbled
- 1 tbsp olive oil
- Salt and pepper to taste

Serves: 2   **Prep time**: 5 min   **Cook time**: 10 min

DIRECTIONS

In a bowl, whisk the eggs until well beaten.

Heat the olive oil in a non-stick skillet over medium heat.

Add the spinach and cook until wilted, about 2 minutes.

Pour the beaten eggs over the spinach and cook until the edges begin to set.

Sprinkle the feta cheese over the eggs, then fold the omelet in half.

Continue cooking until the eggs are fully set, about 2-3 minutes more.

NUTRITIONAL INFORMATION (PER SERVING)

220 calories, 16g protein, 3g carbohydrates, 16g fats, 1g fiber, 375mg cholesterol, 320mg sodium, 40mg magnesium, 300mg potassium.

WHOLE GRAIN PANCAKES

INGREDIENTS

- 1 cup whole wheat flour
- 1 tbsp baking powder
- 1 tbsp flaxseed meal
- 1 cup almond milk
- 1 tbsp honey
- 1 tsp vanilla extract
- 1 egg
- Optional: fresh fruit or nuts for topping

Prep time: 10 min   **Cook time:** 15 min   **Serves:** 4

DIRECTIONS

Whisk flour, baking powder, and flaxseed meal in a bowl.

In another bowl, mix almond milk, honey, vanilla, and egg.

Combine wet and dry ingredients, stirring until just mixed.

Heat a non-stick skillet, lightly coat with cooking spray.

Pour 1/4 cup batter per pancake, cook until bubbles form.

Flip and cook until golden brown.

NUTRITIONAL INFORMATION (PER SERVING)

200 calories, 6g protein, 32g carbohydrates, 6g fats, 5g fiber, 30mg cholesterol, 150mg sodium, 40mg magnesium, 150mg potassium.

CHIA SEED PUDDING

INGREDIENTS

- 1/4 cup chia seeds
- 1 cup unsweetened almond milk
- 1 tsp honey (optional)
- 1/2 teaspoon vanilla extract
- Optional: fresh fruit for topping

Prep time: 5 min   **Setting time:** 4 hours (or overnight)   **Serves:** 2

DIRECTIONS

In a bowl or a jar, mix the chia seeds, almond milk, honey, and vanilla extract.

Stir well to combine, then cover and refrigerate for at least 4 hours or overnight.

Stir again before serving and top with fresh fruit if desired.

NUTRITIONAL INFORMATION (PER SERVING)

150 calories, 5g protein, 20g carbohydrates, 7g fats, 10g fiber, 0mg cholesterol, 50mg sodium, 70mg magnesium, 200mg potassium.

QUINOA BREAKFAST BOWL

INGREDIENTS

- 1 cup cooked quinoa (prepare ahead or cook fresh)
- 1/2 cup unsweetened almond milk
- 1/2 tsp cinnamon
- 1 tbsp maple syrup or honey (optional)
- 1/4 cup fresh berries (e.g., blueberries or raspberries)
- 1/4 cup sliced banana
- 2 tbsp chopped walnuts
- 1 tbsp chia seeds (optional, for extra fiber and omega-3s)

Prep time: 5 min   **Cook time:** 15 min   **Serves:** 2

DIRECTIONS

If cooking fresh, rinse 1/2 cup of raw quinoa and cook in 1 cup of water according to package instructions. After cooking, fluff with a fork and set aside.

In a small saucepan, combine the cooked quinoa, almond milk, cinnamon, and maple syrup (if using). Heat over medium-low heat, stirring occasionally, until warmed through (about 3–5 minutes).

Divide the warmed quinoa mixture between two bowls.

Top each bowl with fresh berries, banana slices, walnuts, and chia seeds.

NUTRITIONAL INFORMATION (PER SERVING)

250 calories, 8g protein, 36g carbohydrates, 8g fats, 6g fiber, 0mg cholesterol, 40mg sodium, 90mg magnesium, 300mg potassium.

MEDITERRANEAN VEGGIE OMELETTE

INGREDIENTS

- 4 large eggs (or egg whites)
- 1/2 cup chopped spinach
- 1/4 cup diced bell peppers
- 1/4 cup diced tomatoes
- 1/4 cup crumbled feta cheese (optional)
- 1 tbsp olive oil
- Pepper to taste

Prep time: 10 min   **Cook time:** 10 min   **Serves:** 2

DIRECTIONS

In a bowl, whisk the eggs and season with pepper.

Heat olive oil in a non-stick skillet over medium heat.

Add the chopped spinach, bell peppers, and tomatoes. Sauté for 2-3 minutes.

Pour the whisked eggs over the veggies and cook until the eggs are set.

Sprinkle with crumbled feta cheese if desired.

NUTRITIONAL INFORMATION (PER SERVING)

220 calories, 15g protein, 5g carbohydrates, 15g fats, 2g fiber, 210mg cholesterol, 250mg sodium, 30mg magnesium, 300mg potassium.

GREEK YOGURT PARFAIT WITH BERRIES

INGREDIENTS

- 1 cup plain Greek yogurt
- 1/2 cup granola (preferably low-sugar)
- 1 cup mixed berries
- 1 tbsp honey (optional)

Prep time: 10 min **Serves:** 2

DIRECTIONS

In two glasses or bowls, layer the Greek yogurt, granola, and mixed berries.

Drizzle with honey if desired.

NUTRITIONAL INFORMATION (PER SERVING)

250 calories, 14g protein, 35g carbohydrates, 7g fats, 5g fiber, 5mg cholesterol, 80mg sodium, 30mg magnesium, 300mg potassium.

WHITE FRITTATA WITH VEGETABLES

INGREDIENTS

- 1/2 cup egg whites (about 4 large eggs' worth)
- 1/4 cup diced bell peppers (red, green, or yellow)
- 1/4 cup chopped spinach
- 2 tbsp diced onion
- 2 tbsp chopped mushrooms
- 1 tsp olive oil
- 1/8 tsp garlic powder
- 1/8 tsp black pepper
- Pinch of salt (optional)

Prep time: 10 min **Cook time:** 15 min **Serves:** 2

DIRECTIONS

Preheat oven to 375°F (190°C).

Heat olive oil in an oven-safe skillet over medium heat. Sauté bell peppers, onions, mushrooms, and garlic powder for 3–4 minutes. Add spinach and cook until wilted.

Whisk egg whites with black pepper and salt, then pour over vegetables. Cook for 2–3 minutes until edges set.

Bake for 8–10 minutes until firm and golden. Cool slightly, slice, and serve warm.

NUTRITIONAL INFORMATION (PER SERVING)

100 calories, 10g protein, 4g carbohydrates, 4g fats, 1g fiber, 0mg cholesterol, 70mg sodium, 15mg magnesium, 150mg potassium.

VEGETABLE, SWEET POTATO, AND BLACK BEAN BREAKFAST BOWL

INGREDIENTS

- 1 medium sweet potato, peeled and diced
- 1 cup cooked black beans
- 1/2 cup diced bell peppers (red or yellow)
- 1/2 cup chopped spinach
- 1/4 cup diced red onion
- 1 tbsp olive oil
- 1/2 tsp cumin
- 1/4 tsp smoked paprika
- 1/8 tsp chili powder (opt.)
- 1/8 tsp black pepper
- 1/8 tsp salt (optional)
- 2 tbsp chopped fresh cilantro (optional)
- 2 tbsp plain unsweetened Greek yogurt (optional)

Prep time: 10 min   **Cook time:** 20 min   **Serves:** 2

DIRECTIONS

Heat 1/2 tbsp olive oil in a skillet over medium heat. Add sweet potatoes, cover, and cook for 8–10 minutes, stirring until tender.

Add remaining oil, bell peppers, onion, and spinach. Stir in spices, black pepper, and salt. Cook for 5–7 minutes until softened.

Mix in black beans and cook for 2 minutes. Serve in bowls with Greek yogurt and cilantro.

NUTRITIONAL INFORMATION (PER SERVING)

250 calories, 8g protein, 40g carbohydrates, 7g fats, 10g fiber, 0mg cholesterol, 200mg sodium, 60mg magnesium, 500mg potassium.

QUINOA BREAKFAST PORRIDGE WITH ALMONDS AND CINNAMON

INGREDIENTS

- 1/2 cup quinoa (uncooked)
- 1 cup unsweetened almond milk (plus extra for serving)
- 1/2 cup water
- 1/2 tsp cinnamon
- 1 tbsp maple syrup or honey (optional)
- 2 tbsp sliced almonds
- 1 tbsp chia seeds (optional, for added fiber and omega-3s)
- 1/4 cup fresh berries or sliced banana (optional, for topping)

Prep time: 5 min   **Cook time:** 15 min   **Serves:** 2

DIRECTIONS

Rinse quinoa under cold water in a fine-mesh sieve.

In a saucepan, combine quinoa, almond milk, water, and cinnamon. Bring to a boil, then simmer on low for 12–15 minutes, stirring occasionally, until tender and liquid is mostly absorbed.

Stir in maple syrup or honey if desired. Serve in bowls with almonds, chia seeds, fruit, and extra almond milk if preferred.

NUTRITIONAL INFORMATION (PER SERVING)

260 calories, 8g protein, 36g carbohydrates, 8g fats, 6g fiber, 0mg cholesterol, 40mg sodium, 90mg magnesium, 300mg potassium.

WHOLE GRAIN ENGLISH MUFFIN WITH PEANUT BUTTER

INGREDIENTS

- 1 whole-grain English muffin, split in half
- 2 tbsp natural peanut butter
- 1/2 medium banana, sliced (optional, for topping)
- 1/2 tsp honey or maple syrup (optional, for sweetness)
- 1/2 tsp chia seeds or flaxseeds (optional, for added fiber and omega-3s)

Prep time: 4 min   **Cook time:** 3 min   **Serves:** 2

DIRECTIONS

Split the whole grain English muffin in half and toast it in a toaster or under a broiler until lightly browned.

Spread 1 tablespoon of peanut butter on each half of the toasted English muffin.

Arrange banana slices evenly over the peanut butter. Drizzle with honey or maple syrup, and sprinkle with chia seeds or flaxseeds if desired.

NUTRITIONAL INFORMATION (PER SERVING)

280 calories, 10g protein, 33g carbohydrates, 13g fats, 6g fiber, 0mg cholesterol, 230mg sodium, 50mg magnesium, 320mg potassium.

SPINACH AND FETA BREAKFAST WRAP (WHOLE WHEAT)

INGREDIENTS

- 2 whole wheat tortillas (8-inch)
- 1 cup fresh spinach, chopped
- 2 large eggs, whisked
- 4 tbsp crumbled feta cheese
- 1 tbsp olive oil or butter
- 1/4 tsp black pepper

Prep time: 10 min   **Cook time:** 7 min   **Serves:** 2

DIRECTIONS

Heat olive oil or butter in a nonstick skillet over medium heat. Sauté spinach for 1–2 minutes until wilted.

Move spinach to one side and pour in whisked eggs. Scramble until cooked, then mix with spinach. Season with black pepper.

Place tortillas flat, add spinach-egg mixture, and top with feta.
Fold sides in and roll tightly to form a wrap.

NUTRITIONAL INFORMATION (PER SERVING)

250 calories, 12g protein, 20g carbohydrates, 12g fats, 3g fiber, 115mg cholesterol, 350mg sodium, 35mg magnesium, 250mg potassium.

BROWN RICE OR QUINOA BOWL WITH AVOCADO, VEGETABLES, AND HUMMUS

INGREDIENTS

- 1 cup cooked quinoa or brown rice (warm or cold)
- 1/2 avocado, sliced
- 1/2 cup hummus (preferably low-sodium)
- 1/2 cup cherry tomatoes, halved
- 1/4 cup shredded carrots
- 1/4 cup cucumber, diced
- 2 tbsp pumpkin seeds (pepitas)
- 1 tbsp olive oil
- 1/2 tsp lemon juice
- 1/8 tsp black pepper
- Optional: A sprinkle of paprika or chili flakes for

Prep time: 15 min   **Serves:** 2

DIRECTIONS

Divide the cooked quinoa or brown rice evenly between two bowls.

Arrange the avocado slices, hummus, cherry tomatoes, shredded carrots, and diced cucumber on top of the base in each bowl.

Sprinkle each bowl with pumpkin seeds. Drizzle with olive oil and lemon juice, and season with black pepper.

Add a sprinkle of paprika or chili flakes for extra flavor.

NUTRITIONAL INFORMATION (PER SERVING)

300 calories, 8g protein, 27g carbohydrates, 18g fats, 7g fiber, 0mg cholesterol, 150mg sodium, 60mg magnesium, 400mg potassium.

TOFU SCRAMBLE WITH VEGETABLES

INGREDIENTS

- 1 block (14 oz) firm tofu, drained and crumbled
- 1 tbsp olive oil
- 1/2 cup diced bell peppers (red or yellow)
- 1/2 cup diced zucchini
- 1/4 cup diced onion
- 1 cup fresh spinach, chopped
- 1/4 tsp turmeric powder
- 1/4 tsp garlic powder
- 1/4 tsp black pepper
- 1 tbsp nutritional yeast (optional, for cheesy flavor)
- 1 tbsp chopped fresh parsley or cilantro

Prep time: 15 min   **Cook time:** 10 min   **Serves:** 2

DIRECTIONS

Drain the tofu and crumble it into small pieces with your hands or a fork. Heat olive oil in a nonstick skillet over medium heat. Sauté onion, bell peppers, and zucchini for 3–4 minutes until softened.

Add crumbled tofu, turmeric, garlic powder, and black pepper. Stir and cook for 5–6 minutes.

Mix in spinach and cook for 1–2 minutes. Add nutritional yeast if desired. Serve on plates, garnished with parsley or cilantro.

NUTRITIONAL INFORMATION (PER SERVING)

220 calories, 15g protein, 10g carbohydrates, 13g fats, 4g fiber, 0mg cholesterol, 30mg sodium, 60mg magnesium, 400mg potassium.

APPLE CINNAMON BAKED OATMEAL

INGREDIENTS

- 2 cups old-fashioned oats
- 1 tsp cinnamon
- 1 tsp baking powder
- 1/2 cup unsweetened almond milk (or any milk of choice)
- 2 large eggs
- 1/4 cup maple syrup or honey
- 1 tsp vanilla extract
- 1 medium apple, diced (about 1 cup)
- 1/4 cup chopped walnuts or pecans (optional)
-

Prep time: 10 min   **Cook time:** 35 min   **Serves:** 6

DIRECTIONS

Preheat the oven to 350°F (175°C) and lightly grease an 8x8-inch baking dish.
In a bowl, mix oats, cinnamon, and baking powder.

In another bowl, whisk almond milk, eggs, maple syrup, and vanilla.
Combine wet and dry ingredients, then stir in apples and nuts if using.
Pour into the dish and bake for 30–35 minutes until golden and set.

Cool for 5 minutes, slice into 6, and serve warm.

NUTRITIONAL INFORMATION (PER SERVING)

180 calories, 5g protein, 27g carbohydrates, 5g fats, 4g fiber, 40mg cholesterol, 10mg sodium, 40mg magnesium, 150mg potassium.

BERRY CHIA SEED PUDDING

INGREDIENTS

- 1/4 cup chia seeds
- 1 cup unsweetened almond milk (or any plant-based milk)
- 1/2 tsp vanilla extract
- 1 tbsp honey or maple syrup (optional, for sweetness)
- 1/2 cup mixed fresh berries (e.g., blueberries, raspberries, or strawberries)
- 1 tbsp sliced almonds or shredded coconut (optional, for topping)

Prep time: 5 min   **Chill time:** 4 hours (or overnight)   **Serves:** 2

DIRECTIONS

In a bowl or jar, whisk chia seeds, almond milk, vanilla extract, and honey or maple syrup if using.

Mix well to prevent clumping.

Cover and refrigerate for at least 4 hours or overnight until thickened.
Once set, divide into two bowls and top with mixed berries, sliced almonds, or shredded coconut if desired.

NUTRITIONAL INFORMATION (PER SERVING)

180 calories, 6g protein, 18g carbohydrates, 9g fats, 10g fiber, 0mg cholesterol, 20mg sodium, 70mg magnesium, 250mg potassium.

HOMEMADE GRANOLA WITH NUTS AND SEEDS

INGREDIENTS

- 2 cups old-fashioned oats
- 1/2 cup chopped almonds
- 1/2 cup chopped walnuts
- 1/4 cup pumpkin seeds (pepitas)
- 1/4 cup sunflower seeds
- 1/4 cup unsweetened shredded coconut (optional)
- 1/3 cup honey or maple syrup
- 1/4 cup olive oil or melted coconut oil
- 1 tsp vanilla extract
- 1/2 tsp cinnamon
- 1/4 tsp salt (optional)

Prep time: 10 min   **Cook time:** 25 min   **Serves:** 8 (1/4 cup per serving)

DIRECTIONS

Preheat oven to 325°F (165°C) and line a baking sheet with parchment paper.

In a bowl, mix oats, almonds, walnuts, pumpkin seeds, sunflower seeds, coconut (if using), cinnamon, and salt.

Whisk honey or maple syrup, oil, and vanilla in a separate bowl.

Combine wet and dry ingredients, stirring well.

Spread on the baking sheet and bake for 20–25 minutes, stirring halfway, until golden.

Cool completely before storing in an airtight container.

NUTRITIONAL INFORMATION (PER SERVING)

210 calories, 5g protein, 22g carbohydrates, 11g fats, 4g fiber, 0mg cholesterol, 30mg sodium, 50mg magnesium, 150mg potassium..

SMOKED SALMON ON WHOLE GRAIN BAGEL WITH AVOCADO

INGREDIENTS

- 2 whole grain bagels, halved and toasted
- 1/2 avocado, mashed
- 4 oz smoked salmon
- 4 thin slices of tomato
- 1/2 cup baby spinach or arugula
- 1/4 tsp black pepper
- Optional: A squeeze of lemon juice and a sprinkle of fresh dill

Prep time: 10 min   **Serves:** 2

DIRECTIONS

Toast the whole grain bagel halves until golden brown.

Mash the avocado in a small bowl and spread it evenly over the toasted bagel halves.

Top each bagel half with smoked salmon, followed by a slice of tomato and a few baby spinach or arugula leaves.

Sprinkle with black pepper. Add a squeeze of lemon juice and a sprinkle of fresh dill, if desired.

NUTRITIONAL INFORMATION (PER SERVING)

310 calories, 17g protein, 35g carbohydrates, 12g fats, 7g fiber, 25mg cholesterol, 530mg sodium, 40mg magnesium, 300mg potassium.

BUCKWHEAT PANCAKES WITH MAPLE SYRUP AND PECANS

INGREDIENTS

- 1 cup buckwheat flour
- 1 tsp baking powder
- 1/4 tsp baking soda
- 1/4 tsp cinnamon
- 1 tbsp ground flaxseed (optional, for added fiber)
- 1 cup almond milk (or another plant-based milk)
- 1 large egg (or a flax egg for vegan option: 1 tbsp ground flaxseed + 3 tbsp water)
- 1 tbsp maple syrup (for the batter)
- 1/2 tsp vanilla extract
- 1/4 cup chopped pecans
- 1/4 cup pure maple syrup

Prep time: 10 min   **Cook time:** 15 min   **Serves:** 4

DIRECTIONS

In a large bowl, whisk buckwheat flour, baking powder, baking soda, cinnamon, and flaxseed (if using).

In another bowl, whisk almond milk, egg, maple syrup, and vanilla. Gradually mix wet ingredients into dry until just combined.
Heat a greased skillet over medium heat. Pour 1/4 cup batter per pancake, cooking 2–3 minutes per side until golden.

Serve warm with pecans and maple syrup.

NUTRITIONAL INFORMATION (PER SERVING)

220 calories, 7g protein, 31g carbohydrates, 8g fats, 5g fiber, 30mg cholesterol, 150mg sodium, 50mg magnesium, 200mg potassium.

MUESLI WITH ALMOND MILK AND FRESH FRUIT

INGREDIENTS

- 1 cup muesli (store-bought or homemade, with oats, nuts, and dried fruit)
- 1 cup unsweetened almond or any plant-based milk
- 1/2 cup fresh mixed fruit (e.g., sliced banana, berries, or diced apple)
- 1 tbsp chia seeds or flaxseeds (optional, for added fiber and omega-3s)
- 1 tbsp honey, date, or maple syrup (optional)

Prep time: 5 min   **Serves:** 2

DIRECTIONS

Divide the muesli evenly between two bowls.

Pour 1/2 cup of almond milk over the muesli in each bowl. Stir gently to combine.

Add the fresh mixed fruit evenly over the top of each bowl.

Sprinkle chia seeds or flaxseeds on top for extra nutrients, and drizzle with honey or maple syrup if desired.

NUTRITIONAL INFORMATION (PER SERVING)

220 calories, 6g protein, 36g carbohydrates, 7g fats, 7g fiber, 0mg cholesterol, 60mg sodium, 50mg magnesium, 250mg potassium.

BAKED MIXED VEGETABLE CHIPS

INGREDIENTS

- 1 medium beet, peeled and thinly sliced
- 1 medium zucchini, thinly sliced
- 1 medium carrot, peeled and thinly sliced
- 1 medium parsnip, peeled and thinly sliced
- 1 tbsp olive oil
- 1/4 tsp smoked paprika (optional)
- 1/4 tsp garlic powder (optional)
- 1/4 tsp black pepper

Prep time: 15 min **Cook time:** 20-30 min **Serves:** 4

DIRECTIONS

Preheat oven to 375°F (190°C) and line two baking sheets with parchment paper.

Thinly slice vegetables into 1/8-inch rounds using a mandoline or sharp knife. Toss slices with olive oil, smoked paprika, garlic powder, and black pepper.

Arrange in a single layer on baking sheets without overlapping. Bake for 20–30 minutes, flipping halfway. Remove chips as they crisp to prevent burning.

Let cool to crisp further, then store in an airtight container.

NUTRITIONAL INFORMATION (PER SERVING)

100 calories, 2g protein, 16g carbohydrates, 3g fats, 3g fiber, 0mg cholesterol, 25mg sodium, 30mg magnesium, 300mg potassium.

STUFFED CHERRY TOMATOES WITH COTTAGE CHEESE

INGREDIENTS

- 16 large cherry tomatoes
- 1/2 cup low-fat cottage cheese
- 1 tbsp fresh parsley, chopped
- 1 tbsp fresh chives, chopped
- 1/4 tsp garlic powder
- 1/4 tsp black pepper
- Optional: 1 tbsp grated Parmesan cheese (for garnish)

Prep time: 15 min **Cook time:** 20-30 min **Serves:** 4

DIRECTIONS

Wash cherry tomatoes and pat dry. Cut off the tops and carefully scoop out seeds and pulp without piercing the shells. Set aside.

In a bowl, mix cottage cheese, parsley, chives, garlic powder, and black pepper until combined.

Fill each tomato with the mixture using a spoon or piping bag.

Sprinkle with Parmesan if desired.

NUTRITIONAL INFORMATION (PER SERVING - 4 STUFFED TOMATOES)

70 calories, 6g protein, 5g carbohydrates, 3g fats, 1g fiber, 5mg cholesterol, 50mg sodium, 15mg magnesium, 200mg potassium.

CELERY STICKS WITH NUT BUTTER

INGREDIENTS

- 8 medium celery stalks
- 1/4 cup natural almond butter (or any nut butter of your choice)
- 1 tbsp chia seeds or flaxseeds (optional, for topping)
- 1 tbsp unsweetened shredded coconut (optional, for topping)

Prep time: 5 min   **Serves:** 4 (2 celery sticks per serving)

DIRECTIONS

Wash the celery stalks thoroughly and pat them dry. Cut each stalk into 4-inch pieces.

Spread about 1/2 tablespoon of almond butter into the groove of each celery stick.

Sprinkle chia seeds, flaxseeds, or shredded coconut on top of the nut butter for added texture and nutrients (optional).

NUTRITIONAL INFORMATION (PER SERVING)

100 calories, 3g protein, 5g carbohydrates, 8g fats, 3g fiber, 0mg cholesterol, 60mg sodium, 30mg magnesium, 150mg potassium.

HOMEMADE GRANOLA CLUSTERS

INGREDIENTS

- 2 cups rolled oats
- 1/2 cup chopped nuts (e.g., walnuts, almonds, pecans)
- 1/4 cup unsweetened shredded coconut
- 1/4 cup chia seeds or flaxseeds
- 1/4 cup honey or maple syrup
- 2 tbsp almond butter or peanut butter
- 2 tbsp olive oil or coconut oil
- 1 tsp vanilla extract
- 1/2 tsp cinnamon

Prep time: 10 min   **Cook time:** 30 min   **Serves:** 4

DIRECTIONS

Preheat oven to 325°F (165°C) and line a baking sheet with parchment paper.

In a bowl, mix oats, nuts, coconut, chia seeds, and cinnamon.

Heat honey (or maple syrup), almond butter, and olive oil over low heat until smooth. Remove from heat and add vanilla.

Pour over dry ingredients, mixing well. Spread on the baking sheet, pressing firmly. Bake for 20–25 minutes, rotating halfway. Avoid stirring for clusters.

Let cool completely, then break into clusters. tore in an airtight container.

NUTRITIONAL INFORMATION (PER SERVING)

180 calories, 5g protein, 20g carbohydrates, 9g fats, 4g fiber, 0mg cholesterol, 0mg sodium, 40mg magnesium, 200mg potassium.

TOMATO AND OLIVE TAPENADE ON CRACKERS

INGREDIENTS

- 1/2 cup cherry tomatoes, finely chopped
- 1/4 cup Kalamata olives, pitted and finely chopped
- 1 tbsp capers, rinsed and chopped (optional)
- 1 tbsp fresh parsley, chopped
- 1 tsp olive oil
- 1 tsp lemon juice
- 1/4 tsp black pepper
- 8 whole-grain crackers

Prep time: 10 min   **Serves:** 4 (2 crackers per serving)

DIRECTIONS

In a mixing bowl, combine chopped cherry tomatoes, Kalamata olives, capers (if using), parsley, olive oil, lemon juice, and black pepper. Mix until well combined.

Spoon 1 tablespoon of the tomato and olive tapenade onto each whole-grain cracker.

NUTRITIONAL INFORMATION (PER SERVING - 2 CRACKERS WITH TAPENADE)

120 calories, 2g protein, 15g carbohydrates, 5g fats, 2g fiber, 0mg cholesterol, 150mg sodium, 15mg magnesium, 120mg potassium.

KALE AND AVOCADO DIP

INGREDIENTS

- 2 cups fresh kale, finely chopped
- 1 ripe avocado
- 1 tbsp lemon juice
- 1 tbsp olive oil
- 1/4 cup Greek yogurt (optional for creaminess)
- 1 garlic clove, minced
- 1/4 tsp black pepper

Prep time: 10 min   **Serves:** 4

DIRECTIONS

Finely chop the kale leaves and massage them with 1/2 tbsp olive oil until softened.

In a food processor, combine avocado, lemon juice, the remaining olive oil, garlic, Greek yogurt (if using), and black pepper. Blend until smooth.

Stir in the chopped kale. Mix until evenly incorporated.

Serve with whole-grain crackers, sliced vegetables, or as a spread for sandwiches.

NUTRITIONAL INFORMATION (PER SERVING)

120 calories, 2g protein, 8g carbohydrates, 9g fats, 4g fiber, 0mg cholesterol, 10mg sodium, 30mg magnesium, 300mg potassium.

ROASTED RED PEPPER AND CHICKPEA DIP

INGREDIENTS

- 1 cup roasted red peppers (jarred, rinsed, or freshly roasted)
- 1 cup canned chickpeas, drained and rinsed
- 2 tbsp olive oil
- 1 tbsp lemon juice
- 1 garlic clove, minced
- 1/2 tsp smoked paprika (optional)
- 1/4 tsp cumin
- 1/4 tsp black pepper

Prep time: 10 min   **Serves:** 4

DIRECTIONS

Add roasted red peppers, chickpeas, olive oil, lemon juice, garlic, smoked paprika, cumin, and black pepper to a food processor. Blend until smooth.

Add 1–2 tablespoons of water if needed to achieve the desired consistency. Adjust salt or spices as needed (optional).

Transfer to a serving bowl and serve with raw vegetable sticks (e.g., carrots, celery, or cucumber), whole-grain crackers, or as a spread for sandwiches.

NUTRITIONAL INFORMATION (PER SERVING)

110 calories, 3g protein, 9g carbohydrates, 7g fats, 2g fiber, 0mg cholesterol, 40mg sodium, 20mg magnesium, 200mg potassium.

GARLIC AND LEMON ROASTED BROCCOLI

INGREDIENTS

- 1 large head of broccoli, cut into florets
- 1 tbsp olive oil
- 2 garlic cloves, minced
- 1 tbsp lemon juice
- 1/4 tsp black pepper

Prep time: 5 min   **Cook time:** 20 min   **Serves:** 4

DIRECTIONS

Preheat the oven to 400°F (200°C) and line a baking sheet with parchment paper.

In a large bowl, toss broccoli florets with olive oil, minced garlic, and black pepper.

Spread the broccoli on the baking sheet and roast for 18–20 min or until tender and slightly crispy. Remove from the oven, drizzle with lemon juice, and toss to combine.

NUTRITIONAL INFORMATION (PER SERVING)

100 calories, 3g protein, 8g carbohydrates, 7g fats, 4g fiber, 0mg cholesterol, 20mg sodium, 30mg magnesium, 300mg potassium.

HONEY-GLAZED CARROTS

INGREDIENTS

- 4 medium carrots, peeled and sliced diagonally
- 1 tbsp olive oil
- 1 tbsp honey
- 1/4 tsp cinnamon (optional)
- 1/4 tsp black pepper

Prep time: 5 min   **Cook time:** 15 min   **Serves:** 4

DIRECTIONS

Heat olive oil in a skillet over medium heat. Add carrots and sauté for 10–12 minutes, stirring occasionally, until tender.

Drizzle honey over the carrots and sprinkle with cinnamon and black pepper. Stir to coat evenly.

Cook for another 2–3 minutes, allowing the honey to glaze the carrots.

NUTRITIONAL INFORMATION (PER SERVING)

120 calories, 1g protein, 16g carbohydrates, 5g fats, 3g fiber, 0mg cholesterol, 25mg sodium, 20mg magnesium, 200mg potassium.

SAUTÉED ZUCCHINI AND MUSHROOMS

INGREDIENTS

- 2 medium zucchinis, sliced
- 1 cup mushrooms, sliced
- 1 tbsp olive oil
- 1 garlic clove, minced
- 1/4 tsp black pepper
- Optional: 1 tbsp fresh parsley, chopped

Prep time: 5 min   **Serves:** 2

DIRECTIONS

Heat olive oil in a large skillet over medium heat. Add minced garlic and cook until fragrant.

Add sliced zucchini and mushrooms to the skillet. Sauté for 7–8 minutes, stirring occasionally, until tender.

Sprinkle with black pepper and toss.

Garnish with fresh parsley and serve warm.

NUTRITIONAL INFORMATION (PER SERVING)

90 calories, 2g protein, 8g carbohydrates, 6g fats, 2g fiber, 0mg cholesterol, 10mg sodium, 25mg magnesium, 250mg potassium.

MEDITERRANEAN CHICKPEA SALAD

INGREDIENTS

- 1 can (15 oz) chickpeas, drained and rinsed
- 1 cup cherry tomatoes, halved
- 1/2 cucumber, diced
- 1/4 red onion, thinly sliced
- 1/4 cup Kalamata olives, pitted and sliced
- 1/4 cup crumbled feta cheese
- 2 tbsp fresh parsley, chopped
- 2 tbsp olive oil
- 1 tbsp lemon juice
- 1/2 tsp dried oregano
- 1/4 tsp black pepper

Prep time: 10 min   **Serves:** 4

DIRECTIONS

Halve the cherry tomatoes, dice the cucumber, slice the red onion, and chop the parsley.

In a large bowl, mix the chickpeas, cherry tomatoes, cucumber, red onion, olives, feta cheese, and parsley.

In a small bowl, whisk together the olive oil, lemon juice, dried oregano, and black pepper.

Pour the dressing over the salad ingredients and toss gently to combine.

NUTRITIONAL INFORMATION (PER SERVING)

210 calories, 7g protein, 22g carbohydrates, 10g fats, 6g fiber, 10mg cholesterol, 310mg sodium, 50mg magnesium, 300mg potassium.

CAULIFLOWER TABOULEH

INGREDIENTS

- 1 small head of cauliflower (about 3 cups, riced)
- 1 cup fresh parsley, finely chopped
- 1/4 cup fresh mint, finely chopped
- 1 cup diced tomatoes
- 1/2 cup diced cucumber
- 1/4 cup red onion, finely diced
- 2 tbsp olive oil
- 2 tbsp lemon juice
- 1/2 tsp ground cumin
- 1/4 tsp black pepper

Prep time: 15 min   **Serves:** 4

DIRECTIONS

Chop cauliflower into florets and pulse in a food processor until rice-like, or use store-bought cauliflower rice.

In a bowl, combine cauliflower rice, parsley, mint, tomatoes, cucumber, and red onion.

Whisk olive oil, lemon juice, cumin, and black pepper in a small bowl.

Pour dressing over the salad and toss well.

Serve immediately or chill for 1–2 hours to enhance flavors.

NUTRITIONAL INFORMATION (PER SERVING)

110 calories, 3g protein, 8g carbohydrates, 7g fats, 3g fiber, 0mg cholesterol, 40mg sodium, 35mg magnesium, 200mg potassium.

RAINBOW VEGGIE SALAD

INGREDIENTS

- 2 cups shredded purple cabbage
- 1 cup diced bell peppers (red, yellow, or orange)
- 1 cup shredded carrots
- 1 cup cherry tomatoes, halved
- 1/2 cup cucumber, diced
- 1/4 cup red onion, thinly sliced
- 2 tbsp chopped fresh parsley or cilantro
- 2 tbsp sunflower seeds or pumpkin seeds
- 2 tbsp olive oil
- 1 tbsp lemon juice
- 1 tsp honey or maple syrup (optional)

Prep time: 15 min **Serves:** 4

DIRECTIONS

Chop or shred the purple cabbage, bell peppers, carrots, cherry tomatoes, cucumber, and red onion.

In a large mixing bowl, add all the vegetables and parsley or cilantro.

In a small bowl, whisk together olive oil, lemon juice, honey or maple syrup (if using), and black pepper.

Pour the dressing over the vegetables and toss gently to coat evenly.

Sprinkle sunflower seeds or pumpkin seeds over the salad for added crunch.

NUTRITIONAL INFORMATION (PER SERVING)

130 calories, 3g protein, 12g carbohydrates, 8g fats, 4g fiber, 0mg cholesterol, 30mg sodium, 40mg magnesium, 250mg potassium.

ZUCCHINI NOODLE SALAD

INGREDIENTS

- 2 medium zucchinis, spiralized into noodles
- 1 cup cherry tomatoes, halved
- 1/2 cup diced cucumber
- 1/4 cup thinly sliced red onion
- 1/4 cup Kalamata olives, sliced
- 2 tbsp crumbled feta cheese (optional)
- 2 tbsp olive oil
- 1 tbsp lemon juice
- 1/2 tsp dried oregano

Prep time: 5 min **Serves:** 2

DIRECTIONS

Spiralize zucchini or use a julienne peeler, then pat dry with a paper towel.
In a bowl, combine zucchini noodles, cherry tomatoes, cucumber, red onion, and olives.
Whisk olive oil, lemon juice, oregano, and black pepper in a small bowl.
Pour dressing over the salad and toss gently.
Top with crumbled feta if desired.
Divide into four bowls and serve immediately.

NUTRITIONAL INFORMATION (PER SERVING)

120 calories, 3g protein, 10g carbohydrates, 8g fats, 3g fiber, 5mg cholesterol, 120mg sodium, 40mg magnesium, 300mg potassium.

CUCUMBER AND DILL SALAD

INGREDIENTS

- 2 large cucumbers, thinly sliced
- 1/4 red onion, thinly sliced
- 2 tbsp fresh dill, chopped
- 2 tbsp olive oil
- 1 tbsp lemon juice or apple cider vinegar
- 1/2 tsp garlic powder
- 1/4 tsp black pepper
- Optional: 1 tsp honey or maple syrup for a touch of sweetness

Prep time: 10 min

Serves: 4

DIRECTIONS

Thinly slice the cucumbers and red onion using a sharp knife or mandoline. In a large bowl, mix the sliced cucumbers, red onion, and chopped dill.

In a small bowl, whisk together olive oil, lemon juice or apple cider vinegar, garlic powder, black pepper, and honey or maple syrup (if using).

Pour the dressing over the cucumber mixture and toss gently until evenly coated. Divide into four bowls and serve immediately or refrigerate for 15–20 minutes for enhanced flavor.

NUTRITIONAL INFORMATION (PER SERVING)

90 calories, 1g protein, 6g carbohydrates, 7g fats, 2g fiber, 0mg cholesterol, 20mg sodium, 20mg magnesium, 250mg potassium.

GREEN SALAD WITH DAIKON RADISH AND CUCUMBER

INGREDIENTS

- 1 medium daikon radish, peeled and julienned (about 2 cups)
- 2 medium cucumbers, thinly sliced
- 2 tbsp black sesame seeds (optional, for garnish)

For the Avocado-Parsley Dressing:
- 1 ripe avocado
- 2 tbsp lemon juice
- 2 tbsp olive oil
- 2 tbsp fresh parsley, chopped
- 1/2 tsp garlic powder
- 1/4 tsp black pepper

Prep time: 15 min

Serves: 4

DIRECTIONS

Julienne the daikon radish and thinly slice the cucumbers, then place them in a large salad bowl.

In a bowl, blend avocado, lemon juice, olive oil, parsley, garlic powder, and black pepper with an immersion blender until smooth.

Toss the salad with the dressing until evenly coated.

Garnish with black sesame seeds, divide into four bowls, and serve immediately.

NUTRITIONAL INFORMATION (PER SERVING)

165 calories, 3g protein, 9g carbohydrates, 14g fats, 4g fiber, 0mg cholesterol, 15mg sodium, 45mg magnesium, 290mg potassium.

BROCCOLI SALAD

INGREDIENTS

- 4 cups of fresh broccoli florets, cut into bite-sized pieces.
- 1/4 cup red onion, diced
- 1/4 cup sunflower seeds or slivered almonds
- 1/4 cup dried cranberries (unsweetened if possible)
- 1/2 cup plain unsweetened Greek yogurt
- 2 tbsp mayonnaise (optional, for creaminess)
- 1 tbsp apple cider vinegar or lemon juice
- 1 tbsp honey, date, or maple syrup (optional)
- 1/4 tsp black pepper

Prep time: 10 min   **Serves:** 4

DIRECTIONS

Wash and chop broccoli into bite-sized florets, then place in a large bowl. Add diced red onion, sunflower seeds or slivered almonds, and dried cranberries.

In a small bowl, whisk Greek yogurt, mayonnaise (if using), lemon juice or vinegar, honey or maple syrup (if using), and black pepper until smooth. Toss the salad with the dressing until evenly coated.
Serve immediately or chill for 30 minutes to enhance flavors.

NUTRITIONAL INFORMATION (PER SERVING)

160 calories, 6g protein, 18g carbohydrates, 8g fats, 4g fiber, 5mg cholesterol, 50mg sodium, 35mg magnesium, 300mg potassium.

GEORGIAN TOMATO AND CUCUMBER SALAD

INGREDIENTS

- 2 large tomatoes, diced
- 2 medium cucumbers, diced
- 1/4 red onion, thinly sliced

For the Dressing:
- 2 tbsp olive oil
- 1 tbsp red wine vinegar (or lemon juice)
- 1/2 tsp ground coriander
- 1/4 tsp black pepper
- 1/4 cup fresh cilantro, chopped
- 1/4 cup fresh parsley, chopped

Prep time: 10 min   **Serves:** 4

DIRECTIONS

Dice the tomatoes and cucumbers, and thinly slice the red onion. Place them in a large salad bowl.

In a small bowl or container, combine olive oil, red wine vinegar (or lemon juice), ground coriander, black pepper, cilantro, parsley, and walnuts.

Use an immersion blender to blend the dressing mixture until smooth and creamy.

Pour the dressing over the prepared vegetables and toss gently to coat all ingredients evenly.

NUTRITIONAL INFORMATION (PER SERVING)

140 calories, 3g protein, 10g carbohydrates, 10g fats, 3g fiber, 0mg cholesterol, 10mg sodium, 30mg magnesium, 250mg potassium.

ASIAN CABBAGE SALAD

INGREDIENTS

- 4 cups shredded green cabbage
- 1 cup shredded purple cabbage
- 1/2 cup shredded carrots
- 1/4 cup chopped green onions
- 1/4 cup chopped cilantro (optional)
- 2 tbsp sesame seeds or chopped peanuts (optional, for garnish)

For the Dressing:

- 3 tbsp soy sauce (or tamari for gluten-free)
- 2 tbsp rice vinegar
- 1 tbsp sesame oil
- 1 tbsp honey, date, or maple syrup (optional)
- 1/2 tsp grated fresh ginger
- 1/2 tsp garlic powder
- 1/8 tsp black pepper

Prep time: 15 min   **Serves:** 4

DIRECTIONS

Shred the green and purple cabbage, carrots, and chop the green onions and cilantro. Combine them in a large mixing bowl.

In a small bowl, whisk together soy sauce, rice vinegar, sesame oil, honey, or maple syrup (if using), grated ginger, garlic powder, and black pepper.

Pour the dressing over the vegetable mixture and toss gently to coat all the ingredients evenly.

Sprinkle sesame seeds or chopped peanuts on top for added crunch.

Divide into four bowls and serve immediately, or refrigerate for 20–30 minutes to allow the flavors to meld.

NUTRITIONAL INFORMATION (PER SERVING)

130 calories, 4g protein, 12g carbohydrates, 7g fats, 4g fiber, 0mg cholesterol, 370mg sodium, 40mg magnesium, 250mg potassium.

AVOCADO AND TOMATO SALAD

INGREDIENTS

- 1 large ripe avocado, diced
- 2 medium tomatoes, diced
- 1/4 red onion, thinly sliced
- 1 hard-boiled egg, peeled and sliced
- 2 tbsp fresh cilantro, chopped

For the Dressing:

- 1 tbsp olive oil
- 1/2 tbsp lemon juice or lime juice
- 1/4 tsp garlic powder
- 1/8 tsp black pepper
- Optional: A pinch of salt

Prep time: 10 min   **Cook time:** 15 min (for boiling the egg)   **Serves:** 2

DIRECTIONS

Place the egg in a saucepan, cover with water, and bring to a boil. Reduce heat and simmer for 9–10 minutes. Transfer to ice water, then peel and slice.

Dice the avocado and tomatoes, thinly slice the red onion, and place in a salad bowl.

Whisk olive oil, lemon or lime juice, garlic powder, and black pepper in a small bowl. Add salt if desired.

Pour dressing over the salad, add cilantro, and toss gently. Top with the sliced egg.

NUTRITIONAL INFORMATION (PER SERVING)

215 calories, 6g protein, 9g carbohydrates, 18g fats, 4g fiber, 95mg cholesterol, 15mg sodium, 35mg magnesium, 365mg potassium.

GEORGIAN EGGPLANT WITH WALNUTS

INGREDIENTS

- 2 medium eggplants
- 1 cup walnuts
- 2 cloves garlic
- 1 tsp ground coriander
- 1/2 tsp ground fenugreek (optional)
- 1/2 tsp paprika
- 1/2 tsp salt (optional)
- 1/4 tsp black pepper
- 1 tbsp white wine vinegar
- 2 tbsp water
- 2 tbsp olive oil (for brushing)
- 1/4 cup pomegranate seeds (for garnish)
- 2 tbsp chopped fresh cilantro (for garnish)

Prep time: 20 min   **Cook time:** 25 min   **Serves:** 4

DIRECTIONS

Preheat the oven to 400°F (200°C).

Slice eggplants lengthwise into 1/4-inch strips, salt lightly, and let sit for 10 minutes before patting dry. Place on a parchment-lined baking sheet, brush with olive oil, and bake for 20-25 minutes, flipping halfway.

Blend walnuts, garlic, spices, vinegar, and water into a paste. Spread on eggplant slices, roll, and garnish with pomegranate seeds and cilantro.

Serve chilled or at room temperature.

NUTRITIONAL INFORMATION (PER SERVING)

210 calories, 5g protein, 13g carbohydrates, 16g fats, 4.5g fiber, 0mg cholesterol, 200mg sodium, 42mg magnesium, 340mg potassium.

ZUCCHINI SALAD WITH TAHINI DRESSING

INGREDIENTS

- 2 medium zucchinis, spiralized or thinly sliced
- 1/2 cup cherry tomatoes, halved
- 1/4 cup red onion, thinly sliced
- 2 tbsp fresh parsley, chopped
- 2 tbsp sunflower seeds or sesame seeds (optional, for garnish)
- For the Tahini Dressing:
- 2 tbsp tahini
- 1 tbsp lemon juice
- 1 tbsp olive oil
- 1/2 tsp garlic powder
- 1/4 tsp cumin powder (optional)
- 2–3 tbsp water (to adjust consistency)
- 1/8 tsp black pepper
- Optional: A pinch of salt to taste

Prep time: 15 min   **Serves:** 4

DIRECTIONS

Use a spiralizer or julienne peeler to create zucchini noodles, or thinly slice the zucchini into ribbons. Place them in a large salad bowl.

Add the cherry tomatoes, red onion, and chopped parsley to the bowl with the zucchini.

In a small bowl, whisk together tahini, lemon juice, olive oil, garlic powder, cumin (if using), and black pepper. Gradually add water, 1 tablespoon at a time, until the dressing reaches your desired consistency. Add salt if desired.

Pour the tahini dressing over the salad and toss gently to coat all the vegetables evenly.

Sprinkle sunflower seeds or sesame seeds over the salad for added crunch and serve immediately.

NUTRITIONAL INFORMATION (PER SERVING)

160 calories, 4g protein, 10g carbohydrates, 12g fats, 3g fiber, 0mg cholesterol, 15mg sodium, 40mg magnesium, 280mg potassium.

SALMON AND AVOCADO SALAD

INGREDIENTS

- 2 cups mixed salad greens (e.g., arugula, spinach, or romaine)
- 1 medium avocado, diced
- 1 cup cooked salmon fillet, flaked (grilled, baked, or pan-seared)
- 1/2 cup cherry tomatoes, halved
- 1/4 red onion, thinly sliced
- 1 tbsp sesame seeds or sunflower seeds (optional)

For the Dressing:
- 2 tbsp olive oil
- 1 tbsp lemon juice
- 1/2 tsp Dijon mustard
- 1/4 tsp garlic powder

Prep time: 10 min　　**Cook time:** 10 min　　**Serves:** 2

DIRECTIONS

Cook the salmon by grilling, baking, or pan-searing until fully done and flaky. Let it cool slightly, then break into bite-sized pieces.

Dice the avocado, halve the cherry tomatoes, and thinly slice the red onion. Combine with salad greens in a large bowl.

Whisk olive oil, lemon juice, Dijon mustard, garlic powder, and black pepper in a small bowl. Add salt if desired.

Add the salmon to the salad, drizzle with dressing, and toss gently to keep the avocado intact.

Sprinkle with sesame or sunflower seeds and serve immediately.

NUTRITIONAL INFORMATION (PER SERVING)

340 calories, 20g protein, 12g carbohydrates, 24g fats, 5g fiber, 60mg cholesterol, 200mg sodium, 40mg magnesium, 450mg potassium.

ARUGULA AND BEET SALAD

INGREDIENTS

- 4 cups fresh arugula
- 2 medium beets, cooked, peeled, and diced or sliced (about 1 cup)
- 1/4 cup crumbled goat cheese or feta cheese (optional)
- 1/4 cup walnuts, toasted and chopped
- 1/4 cup red onion, thinly sliced

For the Dressing:
- 3 tbsp olive oil
- 1 tbsp balsamic vinegar
- 1 tsp honey, date, or maple syrup (optional)
- 1/4 tsp Dijon mustard
- 1/8 tsp black pepper

Prep time: 5 min　**Cook time:** 10 min (if cooking beets fresh)　**Serves:** 4

DIRECTIONS

If using fresh beets, boil or roast them until tender, then peel and dice or slice them. If using pre-cooked beets, dice or slice directly.

Place the arugula in a large salad bowl. Add the cooked beets, red onion, walnuts, and goat cheese or feta cheese (if using).

In a small bowl, whisk together olive oil, balsamic vinegar, honey or maple syrup (if using), Dijon mustard, and black pepper.

Pour the dressing over the salad and lightly toss it to mix.

NUTRITIONAL INFORMATION (PER SERVING)

200 calories, 4g protein, 14g carbohydrates, 15g fats, 4g fiber, 5mg cholesterol, 50mg sodium, 45mg magnesium, 300mg potassium.

MEDITERRANEAN LENTIL SOUP (VEGETARIAN)

INGREDIENTS

- 1/2 cup dried green or brown lentils, rinsed
- 1 tbsp olive oil
- 1 small onion, diced
- 1 garlic clove, minced
- 1 medium carrot, diced
- 1 celery stalk, diced
- 1/2 can (7 oz) diced tomatoes
- 3 cups vegetable broth
- 1/2 tsp ground cumin
- 1/4 tsp smoked paprika
- 1/4 tsp black pepper
- 2 tbsp fresh parsley, chopped (for garnish)

Prep time: 10 min   **Cook time:** 30 min   **Serves:** 4

DIRECTIONS

Heat olive oil in a pot over medium heat. Sauté garlic, onion, celery, and carrot for 5 minutes until softened.

Stir in lentils, cumin, smoked paprika, and black pepper. Cook for 1 minute.

Add tomatoes and broth. Simmer for 25 minutes until lentils are tender.

Garnish with parsley and serve warm.

NUTRITIONAL INFORMATION (PER SERVING)

220 calories, 10g protein, 30g carbohydrates, 7g fats, 8g fiber, 0mg cholesterol, 150mg sodium, 25mg magnesium, 300mg potassium.

CHICKEN AND WILD RICE SOUP

INGREDIENTS

- 1/2 lb boneless, skinless chicken breast
- 1/2 tbsp olive oil
- 1 small onion, diced
- 1 garlic clove, minced
- 1 medium carrot, diced
- 1 celery stalk, diced
- 1/2 cup cooked wild rice
- 3 cups chicken broth
- 1/2 tsp dried thyme
- 1/4 tsp black pepper
- 1 tbsp fresh parsley, chopped

Prep time: 10 min   **Cook time:** 30 min   **Serves:** 4

DIRECTIONS

Heat olive oil in a pot over medium heat. Cook chicken until browned, about 6 minutes. Remove and shred.

In the same pot, sauté onion, garlic, carrot, and celery for 5 minutes.

Add chicken, rice, broth, thyme, and black pepper. Simmer for 20 minutes.

Garnish with parsley and serve.

NUTRITIONAL INFORMATION (PER SERVING)

250 calories, 25g protein, 20g carbohydrates, 6g fats, 3g fiber, 45mg cholesterol, 150mg sodium, 20mg magnesium, 300mg potassium.

BEEF AND BARLEY SOUP (LEAN BEEF)

INGREDIENTS

- 1/2 lb lean beef stew meat, cubed
- 1/2 tbsp olive oil
- 1 small onion, diced
- 1 garlic clove, minced
- 1 medium carrot, diced
- 1 celery stalk, diced
- 1/4 cup pearl barley
- 1/2 can (7 oz) diced tomatoes
- 3 cups beef broth
- 1/2 tsp dried thyme
- 1/4 tsp black pepper

Prep time: 15 min   **Cook time:** 1 hour   **Serves:** 4

DIRECTIONS

Heat olive oil in a pot. Brown beef, then remove.

Sauté onion, garlic, carrot, and celery for 5 minutes.

Add beef, barley, tomatoes, broth, thyme, and pepper. Simmer for 50–60 minutes.

Adjust seasoning and serve warm.

NUTRITIONAL INFORMATION (PER SERVING)

290 calories, 22g protein, 25g carbohydrates, 9g fats, 5g fiber, 45mg cholesterol, 150mg sodium, 20mg magnesium, 300mg potassium.

SPICED CARROT AND GINGER SOUP (VEGETARIAN)

INGREDIENTS

- 1/2 tbsp olive oil
- 1 small onion, diced
- 1 garlic clove, minced
- 1/2 tbsp grated fresh ginger
- 3 large carrots, peeled and chopped
- 2 cups vegetable broth
- 1/4 tsp ground cumin
- 1/8 tsp ground coriander
- 1/8 tsp black pepper
- Optional: 1 tbsp coconut milk

Prep time: 10 min   **Cook time:** 25 min   **Serves:** 4

DIRECTIONS

Heat olive oil in a pot. Sauté garlic, onion, and ginger for 3 minutes.

Stir in carrots, cumin, coriander, and black pepper. Cook for 2 minutes.

Add broth and simmer for 20 minutes until carrots are tender.

Puree the soup with an immersion blender until smooth. Stir in coconut milk if desired.

Serve warm.

NUTRITIONAL INFORMATION (PER SERVING)

180 calories, 3g protein, 24g carbohydrates, 8g fats, 6g fiber, 0mg cholesterol, 100mg sodium, 25mg magnesium, 250mg potassium.

SLOW-COOKED BEEF AND VEGETABLE SOUP

INGREDIENTS

- 1/2 lb lean beef stew meat, cubed
- 1 cup diced potatoes
- 1 medium carrot, sliced
- 1 celery stalk, chopped
- 1/2 cup green beans, chopped
- 1/2 can (7 oz) diced tomatoes
- 3 cups beef broth
- 1/2 tsp dried thyme
- 1/4 tsp garlic powder
- 1/4 tsp black pepper

Prep time: 10 min **Cook time:** 6 hours (slow cooker) **Serves:** 4

DIRECTIONS

Add beef, potatoes, carrot, celery, green beans, tomatoes, broth, thyme, garlic powder, and black pepper to the slow cooker.

Cover and cook on low for 6 hours or until the beef and vegetables are tender.

Adjust seasoning if needed and serve warm.

NUTRITIONAL INFORMATION (PER SERVING)

230 calories, 18g proteir, 20g carbohydrates, 8g fats, 4g fiber, 45mg cholesterol, 150mg sodium, 25mg magnesium, 300mg potassium.

CHICKPEA AND KALE VEGETARIAN SOUP

INGREDIENTS

- 1/2 tbsp olive oil
- 1 small onion, diced
- 1 garlic clove, minced
- 1/2 tsp ground cumin
- 1/8 tsp red pepper flakes (optional)
- 1 can (15 oz) chickpeas, drained and rinsed
- 3 cups vegetable broth
- 1 cup chopped kale (stems removed)
- 1/4 cup diced tomatoes
- 1 tbsp lemon juice

Prep time: 10 min **Cook time:** 20 min **Serves:** 4

DIRECTIONS

Heat olive oil in a pot. Sauté garlic, onion, cumin, and red pepper flakes for 3 minutes until fragrant.

Add chickpeas, broth, kale, and tomatoes. Simmer for 15 minutes until kale is tender.

Stir in lemon juice and adjust the seasoning.

Ladle into bowls and serve warm.

NUTRITIONAL INFORMATION (PER SERVING)

190 calories, 7g protein, 18g carbohydrates, 6g fats, 5g fiber, 0mg cholesterol, 100mg sodium, 20mg magnesium, 250mg potassium.

LEMON CHICKEN AND QUINOA SOUP

INGREDIENTS

- 1/2 lb boneless, skinless chicken breast
- 1/2 tbsp olive oil
- 1 small onion, diced
- 1 garlic clove, minced
- 1 medium carrot, diced
- 1 celery stalk, diced
- 1/4 cup quinoa, rinsed
- 3 cups chicken broth
- 1/2 tsp dried thyme
- 1 tbsp lemon juice
- 1 tbsp fresh parsley, chopped

Prep time: 10 min **Cook time:** 30 min **Serves:** 4

DIRECTIONS

Heat olive oil in a pot over medium heat. Cook chicken until browned and cooked through about 6 minutes. Remove, shred, and set aside.

In the same pot, sauté onion, garlic, carrot, and celery for 5 minutes.

Add broth, quinoa, thyme, and shredded chicken. Simmer for 20 minutes until quinoa is tender.

Stir in lemon juice and parsley.

Serve immediately.

NUTRITIONAL INFORMATION (PER SERVING)

220 calories, 20g protein, 18g carbohydrates, 6g fats, 2g fiber, 45mg cholesterol, 150mg sodium, 20mg magnesium, 300mg potassium.

HEARTY VEGETARIAN MINESTRONE SOUP

INGREDIENTS

- 1/2 tbsp olive oil
- 1 small onion, diced
- 1 garlic clove, minced
- 1 medium carrot, diced
- 1 celery stalk, diced
- 1/2 cup green beans, chopped
- 1/2 can (7 oz) diced tomatoes
- 3 cups vegetable broth
- 1/2 cup cooked small pasta (gluten-free if needed)
- 1/2 cup canned kidney beans, drained and rinsed
- 1/2 tsp dried basil
- 1/4 tsp oregano

Prep time: 15 min **Cook time:** 30 min **Serves:** 4

DIRECTIONS

Heat olive oil in a pot over medium heat. Add onion, garlic, carrot, and celery. Sauté for 5 minutes.

Add green beans, tomatoes, broth, basil, and oregano. Simmer for 20 minutes.

Stir in cooked pasta and kidney beans. Simmer for 5 minutes.

Garnish with parsley or Parmesan cheese, if desired.

NUTRITIONAL INFORMATION (PER SERVING)

210 calories, 6g protein, 35g carbohydrates, 5g fats, 5g fiber, 0mg cholesterol, 100mg sodium, 25mg magnesium, 300mg potassium.

QUINOA AND BLACK BEAN BOWL

INGREDIENTS

- 1 cup quinoa, rinsed
- 2 cups vegetable broth
- 1 can (15 oz) black beans, drained and rinsed
- 1 cup cherry tomatoes, halved
- 1 avocado, diced
- 1/4 cup chopped fresh cilantro
- 1/4 cup lime juice
- 1 tsp cumin
- 1/2 tsp chili powder
- 1/4 tsp black pepper

Prep time: 10 min   **Cook time:** 20 min   **Serves:** 4

DIRECTIONS

Bring vegetable broth to a boil, add quinoa, reduce heat, and simmer for 15 minutes or until the liquid is absorbed. Fluff with a fork.

Dice the avocado, halve the cherry tomatoes, and chop the cilantro.

Divide quinoa into four bowls. Top with black beans, cherry tomatoes, avocado, and cilantro.

Drizzle lime juice and sprinkle cumin, chili powder, and black pepper over each bowl. Serve immediately.

NUTRITIONAL INFORMATION (PER SERVING)

310 calories, 10g protein, 40g carbohydrates, 12g fats, 9g fiber, 0mg cholesterol, 200mg sodium, 50mg magnesium, 500mg potassium.

LENTIL AND SPINACH CURRY

INGREDIENTS

- 1 cup dried lentils (green or brown), rinsed
- 2 cups water or vegetable broth
- 1 tbsp olive oil
- 1 medium onion, diced
- 2 garlic cloves, minced
- 1 tbsp curry powder
- 1/2 tsp turmeric
- 1 can (14 oz) diced tomatoes
- 4 cups fresh spinach
- 1/4 cup coconut milk
- 1/4 tsp salt (optional)

Prep time: 10 min   **Cook time:** 30 min   **Serves:** 4

DIRECTIONS

Simmer lentils in water or broth for 20 minutes until tender. Drain and set aside.

Heat olive oil in a pot over medium heat. Sauté onion and garlic until fragrant. Stir in curry powder and turmeric.

Stir in diced tomatoes and simmer for 5 minutes. Add cooked lentils and spinach. Stir in coconut milk and cook for 5 minutes until spinach wilts. Season with salt if desired.

Serve warm with rice or flatbread.

NUTRITIONAL INFORMATION (PER SERVING)

290 calories, 15g protein, 35g carbohydrates, 10g fats, 8g fiber, 0mg cholesterol, 300mg sodium, 60mg magnesium, 600mg potassium.

SWEET POTATO AND KALE STIR-FRY

INGREDIENTS

- 2 medium sweet potatoes, peeled and cubed
- 1 tbsp olive oil
- 1/2 cup red onion, diced
- 2 garlic cloves, minced
- 4 cups chopped kale, stems removed
- 1/4 tsp smoked paprika
- 1/4 tsp black pepper
- Optional: 1 tbsp lemon juice

Prep time: 10 min   **Cook time:** 20 min   **Serves:** 4

DIRECTIONS

Heat olive oil in a skillet over medium heat. Add sweet potatoes and cook for 10–12 minutes, stirring occasionally.

Push sweet potatoes to one side. Add onion and garlic, sautéing until fragrant.

Stir in kale, smoked paprika, and black pepper. Cover the skillet and cook for 5 minutes, or until the kale is softened.

Drizzle with lemon juice, toss, and serve immediately.

NUTRITIONAL INFORMATION (PER SERVING)

180 calories, 4g protein, 28g carbohydrates, 7g fats, 5g fiber, 0mg cholesterol, 20mg sodium, 50mg magnesium, 400mg potassium.

EGGPLANT AND CHICKPEA STEW

INGREDIENTS

- 1 large eggplant, diced
- 2 tbsp olive oil
- 1 medium onion, diced
- 2 garlic cloves, minced
- 1 can (15 oz) chickpeas, drained and rinsed
- 1 can (14 oz) diced tomatoes
- 1 cup vegetable broth
- 1 tsp smoked paprika
- 1/2 tsp ground cumin
- 1/4 tsp black pepper
- 1/4 cup fresh parsley, chopped

Prep time: 10 min   **Cook time:** 30 min   **Serves:** 4

DIRECTIONS

Heat olive oil in a large pot over medium heat. Add eggplant and cook for 5–7 minutes until softened. Add onion and garlic, sautéing until fragrant.

Stir in diced tomatoes, vegetable broth, smoked paprika, cumin, and black pepper. Simmer for 15 minutes.

Add chickpeas and cook for another 5 minutes.

Garnish with parsley and serve with rice or bread.

NUTRITIONAL INFORMATION (PER SERVING)

220 calories, 7g protein, 27g carbohydrates, 10g fats, 8g fiber, 0mg cholesterol, 300mg sodium, 50mg magnesium, 450mg potassium.

VEGETABLE STIR-FRY WITH BROWN RICE

INGREDIENTS

- 2 cups cooked brown rice
- 1 tbsp sesame oil
- 1 cup broccoli florets
- 1/2 cup sliced bell peppers (red, yellow, or green)
- 1/2 cup sliced carrots
- 1/4 cup snap peas
- 2 tbsp low-sodium soy sauce
- 1 tsp grated fresh ginger
- 1/2 tsp garlic powder
- 1/2 tsp sesame seeds (optional)

Prep time: 10 min **Cook time:** 20 min **Serves:** 4

DIRECTIONS

Wash and slice the vegetables into bite-sized pieces.

Heat sesame oil in a large skillet or wok over medium heat. Add broccoli, carrots, and snap peas, and cook for 5 minutes. Add bell peppers and cook for another 3–4 minutes.

Stir in soy sauce, ginger, and garlic powder. Toss to coat evenly.

Add cooked brown rice to the skillet and stir-fry for 3–4 minutes until heated through.

Sprinkle with sesame seeds and serve immediately.

NUTRITIONAL INFORMATION (PER SERVING)

250 calories, 6g protein, 38g carbohydrates, 7g fats, 5g fiber, 0mg cholesterol, 250mg sodium, 60mg magnesium, 450mg potassium.

SPINACH AND FETA STUFFED PORTOBELLO MUSHROOMS

INGREDIENTS

- 4 large Portobello mushroom caps, stems removed
- 2 cups fresh spinach, chopped
- 1/2 cup crumbled feta cheese
- 1 tbsp olive oil
- 1/2 tsp garlic powder
- 1/4 tsp black pepper

Prep time: 10 min **Cook time:** 15 min **Serves:** 4

DIRECTIONS

Preheat the oven to 375°F (190°C). Line a baking sheet with parchment paper.

Brush the mushroom caps with olive oil and place them on the baking sheet.

Sauté spinach in a small skillet until wilted. Mix in feta cheese, garlic powder, and black pepper.

Spoon the spinach mixture into each mushroom cap. Bake for 12–15 minutes until the mushrooms are tender and the filling is warm.

NUTRITIONAL INFORMATION (PER SERVING)

150 calories, 5g protein, 7g carbohydrates, 10g fats, 2g fiber, 15mg cholesterol, 150mg sodium, 30mg magnesium, 400mg potassium.

WHOLE-WHEAT VEGGIE PIZZA

INGREDIENTS

- 1 whole-wheat pizza crust
- 1/2 cup pizza sauce
- 1/2 cup shredded mozzarella cheese
- 1/4 cup diced bell peppers
- 1/4 cup sliced mushrooms
- 1/4 cup black olives, sliced
- 1/4 cup fresh spinach leaves

Prep time: 10 min   **Cook time:** 15 min   **Serves:** 4

DIRECTIONS

Preheat the oven according to the crust's instructions.

Spread pizza sauce over the crust. Add mozzarella cheese, bell peppers, mushrooms, olives, and spinach.

Bake in the oven for 12–15 minutes or until the crust is crisp and the cheese is melted.

Slice into 4 pieces and serve warm.

NUTRITIONAL INFORMATION (PER SERVING)

220 calories, 8g protein, 25g carbohydrates, 10g fats, 3g fiber, 15mg cholesterol, 250mg sodium, 25mg magnesium, 300mg potassium.

ZUCCHINI NOODLE ALFREDO

INGREDIENTS

- 4 medium zucchinis, spiralized into noodles
- 1 tbsp olive oil
- 1/2 cup unsweetened almond milk
- 1/4 cup grated Parmesan cheese
- 2 tbsp cream cheese (or plant-based alternative)
- 2 garlic cloves, minced
- 1/4 tsp black pepper
- Optional: 1 tbsp chopped fresh parsley (for garnish)

Prep time: 10 min   **Cook time:** 10 min   **Serves:** 4

DIRECTIONS

Spiralize the zucchini into noodles and pat them dry with paper towels to remove excess moisture.

Heat olive oil in a skillet over medium heat. Add garlic and sauté until fragrant. Stir in almond milk, Parmesan, and cream cheese, whisking until smooth.

Add the zucchini noodles to the skillet and toss gently to coat them in the sauce. Cook for 2–3 minutes until heated through but still firm.

NUTRITIONAL INFORMATION (PER SERVING)

150 calories, 6g protein, 10g carbohydrates, 10g fats, 2g fiber, 10mg cholesterol, 150mg sodium, 30mg magnesium, 400mg potassium.

CAULIFLOWER FRIED RICE

INGREDIENTS

- 1 medium head of cauliflower, riced (about 4 cups)
- 1 tbsp sesame oil
- 1/2 cup diced carrots
- 1/2 cup frozen peas
- 1/4 cup diced onion
- 2 garlic cloves, minced
- 2 eggs, beaten (optional, for protein)
- 2 tbsp low-sodium soy sauce
- Optional: 1 tbsp chopped green onions (for garnish)

Prep time: 10 min   **Cook time:** 15 min   **Serves:** 4

DIRECTIONS

Pulse cauliflower in a food processor until it resembles rice.

Heat sesame oil in a skillet over medium heat. Add carrots, peas, and onion, and sauté for 5 minutes.

Push the vegetables to one side. Add the beaten eggs to the other side and scramble until they are cooked through.

Stir in the cauliflower rice, garlic, and soy sauce. Cook for 5–7 minutes until tender.

Garnish with green onions and serve warm.

NUTRITIONAL INFORMATION (PER SERVING)

130 calories, 5g protein, 12g carbohydrates, 7g fats, 3g fiber, 70mg cholesterol, 200mg sodium, 40mg magnesium, 350mg potassium.

CHICKPEA AND SPINACH MIDDLE EAST SHAKSHUKA

INGREDIENTS

- 1 tbsp olive oil
- 1 medium onion, diced
- 2 garlic cloves, minced
- 1 tsp smoked paprika
- 1/2 tsp ground cumin
- 1 can (14 oz) diced tomatoes
- 1 cup cooked chickpeas (or canned, drained and rinsed)
- 4 cups fresh spinach
- 4 large eggs
- Optional: 1/4 cup crumbled feta (for garnish)

Prep time: 10 min   **Cook time:** 20 min   **Serves:** 4

DIRECTIONS

Heat olive oil in a skillet over medium heat. Add onion and garlic, sautéing until soft. Stir in smoked paprika and cumin.

Pour in diced tomatoes and add chickpeas. Simmer for 5 minutes.

Stir in fresh spinach and cook until wilted.

Make 4 small wells in the sauce. Crack an egg into each well, cover the skillet, and cook for 5–7 minutes or until the egg whites are set.

Sprinkle with feta (if using) and serve with bread or rice.

NUTRITIONAL INFORMATION (PER SERVING)

220 calories, 12g protein, 20g carbohydrates, 9g fats, 6g fiber, 190mg cholesterol, 250mg sodium, 60mg magnesium, 400mg potassium.

STUFFED BELL PEPPERS

INGREDIENTS

- 4 large bell peppers, tops removed and seeds scooped out
- 1 cup cooked quinoa
- 1 cup cooked black beans
- 1/2 cup diced tomatoes
- 1/4 cup corn kernels (optional)
- 1 tsp chili powder
- 1/2 tsp cumin
- 1/4 tsp black pepper
- 1/2 cup shredded cheese (optional, for topping)

Prep time: 15 min   **Cook time:** 35 min   **Serves:** 4

DIRECTIONS

Preheat the oven to 375°F (190°C).

In a bowl, mix cooked quinoa, black beans, diced tomatoes, corn (if using), chili powder, cumin, and black pepper.

Fill each bell pepper with the quinoa mixture. Place the peppers upright in a baking dish.

Cover the dish with foil and bake for 25 minutes. Remove the foil, sprinkle cheese on top (if using), and bake for another 10 minutes.

Let cool slightly and serve warm.

NUTRITIONAL INFORMATION (PER SERVING)

190 calories, 8g protein, 28g carbohydrates, 4g fats, 6g fiber, 5mg cholesterol, 150mg sodium, 50mg magnesium, 400mg potassium.

TEMPEH TACOS

INGREDIENTS

- 1 block (8 oz) tempeh, crumbled
- 1 tbsp olive oil
- 1/2 cup diced onion
- 1 garlic clove, minced
- 1 tsp chili powder
- 1/2 tsp cumin
- 1/2 tsp smoked paprika
- 1/4 cup tomato sauce
- 8 small corn tortillas
- Optional toppings: shredded lettuce, diced tomatoes, avocado slices, or salsa

Prep time: 10 min   **Cook time:** 15 min   **Serves:** 2 (8 tacos)

DIRECTIONS

Heat olive oil in a skillet over medium heat. Add the onion and garlic, and sauté until softened. Stir in the crumbled tempeh.

Sprinkle chili powder, cumin, and smoked paprika over the tempeh. Stir to coat evenly. Pour in the tomato sauce and mix well. Simmer for 5 minutes until heated through.

Warm the tortillas. Divide the tempeh mixture among them and top with desired toppings.

Serve immediately with a side of lime wedges.

NUTRITIONAL INFORMATION (PER SERVING)

220 calories, 11g protein, 20g carbohydrates, 10g fats, 4g fiber, 0mg cholesterol, 150mg sodium, 40mg magnesium, 300mg potassium.

ROASTED VEGETABLE AND CHICKPEA SALAD

INGREDIENTS

Prep time: 10 min   **Cook time:** 30 min   **Serves:** 4

- 2 cups diced sweet potato
- 1 cup broccoli florets
- 1 cup cherry tomatoes
- 1 can (15 oz) chickpeas, drained and rinsed
- 2 tbsp olive oil
- 1 tsp smoked paprika
- 1/2 tsp garlic powder
- 1/4 tsp black pepper
- 4 cups mixed salad greens
- 2 tbsp balsamic vinaigrette (optional)

DIRECTIONS

Preheat oven to 400°F (200°C). Toss sweet potato, broccoli, cherry tomatoes, and chickpeas with olive oil, smoked paprika, garlic powder, and black pepper. Spread on a baking sheet and roast for 25–30 minutes, tossing halfway through.

Divide mixed greens into bowls. Top with roasted vegetables and chickpeas. Drizzle with balsamic vinaigrette if desired and serve immediately.

NUTRITIONAL INFORMATION (PER SERVING)

250 calories, 7g protein, 36g carbohydrates, 9g fats, 8g fiber, 0mg cholesterol, 120mg sodium, 50mg magnesium, 500mg potassium.

MUSHROOM STROGANOFF

INGREDIENTS

Prep time: 10 min   **Cook time:** 20 min   **Serves:** 4

- 1 tbsp olive oil
- 1 medium onion, diced
- 2 garlic cloves, minced
- 3 cups sliced mushrooms (e.g., cremini or button)
- 1/2 tsp smoked paprika
- 1/4 tsp black pepper
- 1 cup vegetable broth
- 1/2 cup plain unsweetened Greek yogurt or plant-based alternative
- 2 cups cooked pasta (gluten-free optional)
- Optional: 2 tbsp chopped

DIRECTIONS

Heat olive oil in a skillet over medium heat. Add onion and garlic, sautéing until soft. Add mushrooms, smoked paprika, and black pepper. Cook for 5–7 minutes.

Pour in the vegetable broth and simmer for 5 minutes.

Reduce heat and stir in Greek yogurt until the sauce is creamy. Do not boil.

Toss the sauce with cooked pasta.

Divide into bowls, garnish with parsley, and serve immediately.

NUTRITIONAL INFORMATION (PER SERVING)

280 calories, 10g protein, 40g carbohydrates, 8g fats, 4g fiber, 5mg cholesterol, 120mg sodium, 40mg magnesium, 350mg potassium.

VEGAN LENTIL SLOPPY JOES

INGREDIENTS

- 1 cup cooked lentils (or canned, drained and rinsed)
- 1 tbsp olive oil
- 1/2 cup diced onion
- 1/2 cup diced bell pepper
- 1/2 cup tomato sauce
- 1 tbsp tomato paste
- 1 tbsp maple syrup
- 1/2 tsp smoked paprika
- 1/4 tsp cumin
- 4 whole-grain buns

Prep time: 10 min   **Cook time:** 20 min   **Serves:** 4

DIRECTIONS

Heat olive oil in a skillet over medium heat. Sauté onion and bell pepper until soft.

Add cooked lentils, tomato sauce, tomato paste, maple syrup, smoked paprika, and cumin. Simmer for 10 minutes, stirring occasionally.

Spoon the lentil mixture onto whole-grain buns.

Serve warm with a side of salad or veggies.

NUTRITIONAL INFORMATION (PER SERVING)

280 calories, 10g protein, 45g carbohydrates, 6g fats, 7g fiber, 0mg cholesterol, 200mg sodium, 40mg magnesium, 450mg potassium.

VEGETABLE STUFFED ZUCCHINI BOATS

INGREDIENTS

- 4 medium zucchinis, halved lengthwise and scooped out
- 1 tbsp olive oil
- 1/2 cup diced tomatoes
- 1/2 cup cooked quinoa
- 1/4 cup shredded mozzarella cheese (optional)
- 1/4 tsp garlic powder
- 1/4 tsp black pepper
- 1 tbsp chopped basil (optional, for garnish)

Prep time: 15 min   **Cook time:** 25 min   **Serves:** 4

DIRECTIONS

Preheat the oven to 375°F (190°C).

Scoop out the zucchini flesh and set the shells on a baking sheet.

In a skillet, heat olive oil. Add diced tomatoes, quinoa, garlic powder, and black pepper. Cook for 5 minutes.

Spoon the mixture into the zucchini shells. Top with mozzarella if desired.

Bake for 20–25 minutes until the zucchini is tender.

Garnish with basil and serve warm.

NUTRITIONAL INFORMATION (PER SERVING)

150 calories, 5g protein, 14g carbohydrates, 8g fats, 3g fiber, 5mg cholesterol, 120mg sodium, 30mg magnesium, 300mg potassium.

THAI PEANUT NOODLES

INGREDIENTS

For the Noodles:

- 8 oz rice noodles or spaghetti (gluten-free if needed)
- 1 cup shredded carrots
- 1 cup bell peppers, thinly sliced (red, yellow, or green)
- 1/4 cup chopped green onions
- 2 tbsp chopped cilantro (optional, for garnish)
- 1 tbsp sesame seeds (optional, for garnish)

For the Peanut Sauce:

- 1/3 cup natural peanut butter
- 2 tbsp soy sauce (or tamari for gluten-free)
- 1 tbsp rice vinegar
- 1 tbsp lime juice
- 1 tbsp honey or maple syrup (optional, for sweetness)
- 1 tsp sesame oil
- 1/2 tsp grated fresh ginger
- 1/4 tsp garlic powder
- 2–3 tbsp warm water (to adjust consistency)

Prep time: 10 min   **Cook time:** 10 min   **Serves:** 4

DIRECTIONS

Cook rice noodles according to the package instructions. Drain and set aside.

In a small bowl, whisk together peanut butter, soy sauce, rice vinegar, lime juice, honey or maple syrup (if using), sesame oil, ginger, garlic powder, and warm water until smooth and creamy.

If you prefer softened vegetables, sauté carrots and bell peppers in a skillet for 2–3 minutes over medium heat with a splash of sesame oil. Otherwise, leave them raw for a crunchier texture.

Toss the cooked noodles with the peanut sauce until well coated. Add the carrots, bell peppers, and green onions, and toss to combine.

Divide into four bowls and top with chopped cilantro and sesame seeds, if desired. Serve immediately.

NUTRITIONAL INFORMATION (PER SERVING)

350 calories, 10g protein, 50g carbohydrates, 12g fats, 5g fiber, 0mg cholesterol, 600mg sodium, 50mg magnesium, 300mg potassium.

SLOW-COOKED MEDITERRANEAN CHICKEN STEW

INGREDIENTS

- 1 lb boneless, skinless chicken breast or thighs, cut into chunks
- 1 tbsp olive oil
- 1 medium onion, diced
- 2 garlic cloves, minced
- 1 red bell pepper, chopped
- 1 zucchini, chopped
- 1 can (14 oz) diced tomatoes (no salt added)
- 1/2 cup low-sodium chicken broth
- 1/2 cup canned chickpeas, drained and rinsed
- 1/4 cup Kalamata olives, sliced
- 1 tsp dried oregano
- 1/2 tsp smoked paprika
- 1/4 tsp black pepper
- 1 tbsp fresh parsley,

Prep time: 15 min   **Cook time:** 4–6 hours (slow cooker)   **Serves:** 4

DIRECTIONS

Heat olive oil in a skillet over medium heat. Add onion and garlic, sautéing for 2–3 minutes until fragrant.

Transfer onion and garlic to the slow cooker. Add chicken, bell pepper, zucchini, diced tomatoes, chicken broth, chickpeas, olives, oregano, smoked paprika, and black pepper. Stir to combine.

Cover and cook on low for 6 hours or on high for 4 hours, until the chicken is tender and flavors meld.

Garnish with fresh parsley and serve warm with whole-grain rice or quinoa.

NUTRITIONAL INFORMATION (PER SERVING)

280 calories, 32g protein, 22g carbohydrates, 10g fats, 5g fiber, 75mg cholesterol, 350mg sodium, 50mg magnesium, 550mg potassium.

ROSEMARY AND GARLIC ROAST CHICKEN

INGREDIENTS

- 1 lb bone-in, skinless chicken thighs or breasts
- 1 tbsp olive oil
- 2 garlic cloves, minced
- 1 tbsp fresh rosemary leaves chopped (or 1 tsp dried rosemary)
- 1 tsp lemon juice
- 1/2 tsp black pepper
- 1/2 tsp paprika
- 1/4 tsp garlic powder

Prep time: 10min   **Cook time:** 45 min   **Serves:** 4

DIRECTIONS

Preheat the oven to 400°F (200°C) and line a baking dish with parchment paper. In a small bowl, mix olive oil, minced garlic, rosemary, lemon juice, black pepper, paprika, and garlic powder.

Place chicken in the baking dish and coat evenly with the seasoning mixture. Bake for 40–45 minutes, or until the chicken reaches an internal temperature of 165°F (75°C) and is golden brown.

Let rest for 5 min before serving. Enjoy with roasted vegetables or a side salad.

NUTRITIONAL INFORMATION (PER SERVING)

260 calories, 32g protein, 2g carbohydrates, 13g fats, 0g fiber, 85mg cholesterol, 200mg sodium, 40mg magnesium, 450mg potassium.

LEAN BEEF AND VEGETABLE STIR-FRY

INGREDIENTS

- 1 lb lean beef (flank steak or sirloin), sliced thinly
- 1 tbsp olive oil
- 2 garlic cloves, minced
- 1 tsp fresh ginger, grated
- 1 red bell pepper, sliced
- 1 cup broccoli florets
- 1 medium carrot, julienned
- 1/2 cup snap peas
- 2 tbsp low-sodium soy sauce
- 1 tbsp rice vinegar
- 1/2 tsp black pepper
- 1/4 tsp red pepper flakes (optional)
- 1 tsp sesame seeds

Prep time: 10 min   **Cook time:** 15 min   **Serves:** 4

DIRECTIONS

Mix soy sauce, rice vinegar, black pepper, and red pepper flakes (if using) in a small bowl.

Heat 1/2 tbsp olive oil in a skillet over medium-high heat. Stir-fry sliced beef for 3–4 minutes until browned, then set aside.

Add remaining oil, then stir-fry garlic, ginger, bell pepper, broccoli, carrot, and snap peas for 5–6 minutes.

Return beef, add sauce, and cook for 2–3 minutes until coated.

Garnish with sesame seeds (if using) and serve with brown rice or quinoa.

NUTRITIONAL INFORMATION (PER SERVING)

290 calories, 30g protein, 18g carbohydrates, 12g fats, 4g fiber, 70mg cholesterol, 300mg sodium, 50mg magnesium, 500mg potassium.

TURKEY AND QUINOA MEATLOAF

INGREDIENTS

- 1 lb lean ground turkey
- 1/2 cup cooked quinoa
- 1 small onion, finely diced
- 2 garlic cloves, minced
- 1 small carrot, grated
- 1 egg
- 1 tbsp low-sodium soy sauce or coconut aminos
- 1/2 tsp black pepper
- 1/2 tsp dried oregano
- 1/4 tsp smoked paprika
- 1 tbsp tomato paste

Prep time: 15 min   **Cook time:** 45 min   **Serves:** 4

DIRECTIONS

Preheat to 375°F (190°C) and line a loaf pan with parchment paper.

In a large bowl, mix ground turkey, cooked quinoa, onion, garlic, grated carrot, egg, soy sauce, black pepper, oregano, smoked paprika, and tomato paste until well combined.

Transfer the mixture to the loaf pan, pressing it down evenly. Bake for 40–45 minutes, or until the internal temperature reaches 165°F (74°C). Let rest for 5 minutes before slicing.

Slice and serve warm with a side of roasted vegetables or a leafy green salad.

NUTRITIONAL INFORMATION (PER SERVING)

260 calories, 30g protein, 15g carbohydrates, 9g fats, 2g fiber, 85mg cholesterol, 280mg sodium, 45mg magnesium, 400mg potassium.

SESAME GINGER TURKEY MEATBALLS

INGREDIENTS

For the Meatballs:

- 1 lb lean ground turkey
- 1/4 cup whole wheat breadcrumbs (or almond flour for gluten-free)
- 1 egg
- 2 garlic cloves, minced
- 1 tbsp fresh ginger, grated
- 1 tbsp low-sodium soy sauce or coconut aminos
- 1/2 tsp black pepper
- 1/2 tsp sesame oil

For the Sauce:

- 2 tbsp low-sodium soy sauce or coconut aminos
- 1 tbsp rice vinegar
- 1 tbsp honey or maple syrup
- 1 tsp sesame oil
- 1/2 tsp cornstarch (optional, for thickening)
- 1 tsp sesame seeds (for garnish)
- 1 tbsp chopped green onions

Prep time: 15 min   **Cook time:** 20 min   **Serves:** 4 (16 meatballs)

DIRECTIONS

Preheat oven to 400°F (200°C) and line a baking sheet.

Mix turkey, breadcrumbs, egg, garlic, ginger, soy sauce, pepper, and sesame oil.

Form into 1-inch meatballs (16) and bake for 18–20 minutes (165°F/74°C).

Simmer soy sauce, vinegar, honey, sesame oil, and cornstarch for 2–3 minutes.

Toss meatballs in sauce. Garnish and serve.

NUTRITIONAL INFORMATION (PER SERVING - 4 MEATBALLS WITH SAUCE)

240 calories, 26g protein, 10g carbohydrates, 10g fats, 1g fiber, 85mg cholesterol, 280mg sodium, 40mg magnesium, 350mg potassium.

HONEY MUSTARD GLAZED PORK TENDERLOIN

INGREDIENTS

- 1 lb pork tenderloin, trimmed
- 1 tbsp olive oil
- 2 tbsp Dijon mustard
- 1 tbsp honey
- 1 garlic clove, minced
- 1/2 tsp black pepper
- 1/2 tsp dried thyme
- 1/4 tsp smoked paprika

Prep time: 10 min   **Cook time:** 25 min   **Serves:** 4

DIRECTIONS

Preheat oven to 400°F (200°C) and line a baking sheet.

Mix Dijon mustard, honey, garlic, black pepper, thyme, and smoked paprika in a bowl.

Rub pork with olive oil and coat with the glaze. Roast for 20–25 minutes until internal temp reaches 145°F (63°C). Let rest for 5 minutes. Slice and serve with roasted veggies or quinoa.

NUTRITIONAL INFORMATION (PER SERVING)

250 calories, 32g protein, 8g carbohydrates, 9g fats, 0g fiber, 85mg cholesterol, 270mg sodium, 40mg magnesium, 450mg potassium.

GREEK YOGURT MARINATED GRILLED CHICKEN

INGREDIENTS

- 1 lb boneless, skinless chicken breasts (about 4 small fillets)
- 1/2 cup plain Greek yogurt (low-fat or non-fat)
- 1 tbsp olive oil
- 1 tbsp lemon juice
- 2 garlic cloves, minced
- 1 tsp dried oregano
- 1/2 tsp black pepper
- 1/4 tsp smoked paprika

Prep time: 10 min   **Marinate time:** 2 hours   **Cook time:** 15 min   **Serves:** 4

DIRECTIONS

Mix Greek yogurt, olive oil, lemon juice, garlic, oregano, black pepper, and smoked paprika in a bowl.

Coat chicken fillets with the marinade, cover, and refrigerate for at least 2 hours or overnight.

Heat a grill over medium-high and oil the grates.

Remove excess marinade and grill chicken for 6–7 minutes per side until 165°F (75°C).

Rest, slice, and serve with veggies or salad.

NUTRITIONAL INFORMATION (PER SERVING)

260 calories, 38g protein, 6g carbohydrates, 9g fats, 0g fiber, 85mg cholesterol, 200mg sodium, 45mg magnesium, 450mg potassium.

CUMIN AND LIME GRILLED FLANK STEAK

INGREDIENTS

- 1 lb flank steak
- 2 tbsp olive oil
- 2 tbsp lime juice
- 2 garlic cloves, minced
- 1 tsp ground cumin
- 1/2 tsp smoked paprika
- 1/2 tsp black pepper
- 1/4 tsp red pepper flakes (optional)
- 1 tbsp fresh cilantro, chopped (for garnish)

Prep time: 10 min   **Marinate time:** 1 hour   **Cook time:** 10 min   **Serves:** 4

DIRECTIONS

Mix olive oil, lime juice, garlic, cumin, smoked paprika, black pepper, and red pepper flakes (if using).

Coat flank steak with marinade, cover, and refrigerate for 1–4 hours.

Heat a grill over medium-high and oil the grates.

Remove excess marinade and grill steak for 4–5 minutes per side until desired doneness.

Rest for 5 minutes, slice thinly, and serve with veggies or quinoa salad.

NUTRITIONAL INFORMATION (PER SERVING)

290 calories, 36g protein, 4g carbohydrates, 15g fats, 0g fiber, 85mg cholesterol, 220mg sodium, 50mg magnesium, 500mg potassium.

GARLIC & YOGURT BRAISED GEORGIAN CHKMERULI CHICKEN

INGREDIENTS

- 1 lb boneless, skinless chicken thighs (or breast)
- 1 tbsp olive oil
- 3 garlic cloves, minced
- 1/2 cup low-fat Greek yogurt
- 1/2 cup low-sodium chicken broth
- 1 tbsp lemon juice
- 1/2 tsp black pepper
- 1/2 tsp ground coriander
- 1/4 tsp smoked paprika (optional)
- 1 tbsp fresh cilantro or parsley, chopped (for garnish)

Prep time: 15 min   **Cook time:** 30 min   **Serves:** 4

DIRECTIONS

Heat olive oil in a large skillet over medium-high heat. Sear chicken for 3–4 minutes per side until golden brown. Remove and set aside.

In the same pan, sauté garlic for 1 minute. Stir in chicken broth, Greek yogurt, lemon juice, black pepper, coriander, and smoked paprika. Mix well.

Return the chicken to the pan, cover, and simmer for 15–20 minutes until tender and cooked through.

Garnish with fresh cilantro or parsley and serve with whole grains like brown rice or quinoa.

NUTRITIONAL INFORMATION (PER SERVING)

280 calories, 35g protein, 6g carbohydrates, 12g fats, 0g fiber, 90mg cholesterol, 180mg sodium, 40mg magnesium, 450mg potassium.

COCONUT LIME GRILLED CHICKEN THIGHS

INGREDIENTS

- 1 lb boneless, skinless chicken thighs
- 1/2 cup light coconut milk
- 2 tbsp lime juice
- 1 tsp lime zest
- 1 tbsp olive oil
- 2 garlic cloves, minced
- 1 tsp ground cumin
- 1/2 tsp black pepper
- 1/4 tsp red pepper flakes (optional)
- 1 tbsp fresh cilantro, chopped (for garnish)

Prep time: 10 min   **Marinate time:** 1 hour   **Cook time:** 15 min   **Serves:** 4

DIRECTIONS

In a bowl, whisk together coconut milk, lime juice, lime zest, olive oil, garlic, cumin, black pepper, and red pepper flakes (if using).

Place chicken thighs in a resealable bag or dish, pour the marinade over them, and coat evenly. Cover and refrigerate for at least 1 hour (or up to overnight).

Heat a grill or grill pan over medium-high heat and lightly oil the grates. Remove excess marinade and grill chicken for 6–7 minutes per side, until fully cooked (internal temperature of 165°F/75°C).

Let rest for a few min, garnish with fresh cilantro, and serve with quinoa, brown rice, or grilled vegetables.

NUTRITIONAL INFORMATION (PER SERVING)

320 calories, 35g protein, 6g carbohydrates, 18g fats, 1g fiber, 90mg cholesterol, 250mg sodium, 45mg magnesium, 500mg potassium.

SPICED LENTIL AND GROUND TURKEY SKILLET

INGREDIENTS

- 1 lb lean ground turkey
- 1 tbsp olive oil
- 1 small onion, diced
- 2 garlic cloves, minced
- 1 tsp ground cumin
- 1/2 tsp smoked paprika
- 1/2 tsp ground coriander
- 1/4 tsp black pepper
- 1/4 tsp red pepper flakes (optional)
- 1 cup cooked lentils (green or brown)
- 1/2 cup low-sodium diced tomatoes
- 1/2 cup low-sodium chicken or vegetable broth
- 1 cup baby spinach, chopped
- 1 tbsp fresh parsley, chopped (for garnish)
-

Prep time: 10 min   **Cook time:** 25 min   **Serves:** 4

DIRECTIONS

Heat olive oil in a skillet over medium heat. Sauté onion and garlic for 3 min until soft. Add turkey and cook for 5–7 minutes, breaking it up until browned.

Stir in cumin, smoked paprika, coriander, black pepper, and red pepper flakes. Cook for 1 min.

Add lentils, tomatoes, and broth. Simmer for 10 minutes.

Stir in spinach and cook for 2 minutes.

Garnish with parsley and serve with quinoa or rice.

NUTRITIONAL INFORMATION (PER SERVING)

320 calories, 34g protein, 28g carbohydrates, 10g fats, 7g fiber, 70mg cholesterol, 280mg sodium, 50mg magnesium, 500mg potassium.

BALSAMIC GLAZED TURKEY BREAST

INGREDIENTS

- 1 lb boneless, skinless turkey breast
- 2 tbsp balsamic vinegar
- 1 tbsp olive oil
- 1 tbsp honey or maple syrup
- 1 garlic clove, minced
- 1/2 tsp dried thyme
- 1/2 tsp black pepper
- 1/4 tsp smoked paprika

Prep time: 10 min   **Cook time:** 40 min   **Serves:** 2

DIRECTIONS

Preheat to 375°F (190°C) and line a baking dish with parchment paper.

In a small bowl, whisk together balsamic vinegar, olive oil, honey, garlic, thyme, black pepper, and smoked paprika.

Place turkey breast in the baking dish and brush evenly with the balsamic glaze. Let marinate for 10 minutes (optional for enhanced flavor).

Roast for 35–40 minutes, basting with glaze halfway through, until the internal temperature reaches 165°F (75°C). Let rest for 5 minutes before slicing. Serve with a side of roasted vegetables or quinoa.

NUTRITIONAL INFORMATION (PER SERVING)

230 calories, 34g protein, 8g carbohydrates, 6g fats, 0g fiber, 85mg cholesterol, 220mg sodium, 45mg magnesium, 450mg potassium.

TERIYAKI GLAZED CHICKEN LETTUCE WRAPS

INGREDIENTS

For the Chicken Filling:
- 1 lb ground or finely diced chicken breast
- 1 tbsp olive oil
- 2 garlic cloves, minced
- 1 tsp fresh ginger, grated
- 1/2 cup shredded carrots
- 1/2 cup red bell pepper, finely chopped
- 2 green onions, chopped
- 8 large lettuce leaves (butter lettuce or romaine)

For the Teriyaki Glaze:
- 2 tbsp low-sodium soy sauce or coconut aminos
- 1 tbsp rice vinegar
- 1 tbsp honey or maple syrup
- 1 tsp sesame oil
- 1/2 tsp cornstarch (optional, for thickening)
- 1 tsp sesame seeds (for garnish)

Prep time: 10 min   **Cook time:** 15 min   **Serves:** 4 (8 wraps)

DIRECTIONS

In a small bowl, whisk together soy sauce, rice vinegar, honey, sesame oil, and cornstarch (if using). Set aside.

Heat olive oil in a skillet over medium heat. Add ginger and garlic, sautéing for 1 minute until they get fragrant. Add ground chicken and cook for 5–7 minutes, breaking it apart until browned.

Stir in carrots, bell pepper, and teriyaki glaze. Cook for 3–4 minutes until the vegetables soften and the sauce thickens. Stir in green onions.

Spoon the chicken mixture into lettuce leaves and sprinkle with sesame seeds.

Enjoy immediately as a light and flavorful meal.

NUTRITIONAL INFORMATION (PER SERVING - 2 WRAPS)

250 calories, 28g protein, 14g carbohydrates, 9g fats, 2g fiber, 70mg cholesterol, 280mg sodium, 40mg magnesium, 400mg potassium.

SALMON BAKED WITH GARLIC AND HERBS

INGREDIENTS

- 2 salmon fillets (5 oz each)
- 1 tbsp olive oil
- 2 garlic cloves, minced
- 1 tbsp lemon juice
- 1/2 tsp dried oregano
- 1/2 tsp dried thyme
- 1/4 tsp black pepper
- 1 tbsp fresh parsley, chopped (for garnish)
- 2 lemon slices (for serving)

Prep time: 10 min   **Cook time:** 15 min   **Serves:** 2

DIRECTIONS

Preheat to 400°F (200°C) and line a baking sheet with parchment paper.

In a small bowl, mix olive oil, minced garlic, lemon juice, oregano, thyme, and black pepper.

Place salmon fillets on the baking sheet and brush evenly with the garlic-herb mixture.

Bake for 12–15 minutes or until the salmon flakes easily with a fork.

Garnish with parsley and serve with lemon slices.

NUTRITIONAL INFORMATION (PER SERVING)

280 calories, 30g protein, 2g carbohydrates, 18g fats, 0g fiber, 70mg cholesterol, 80mg sodium, 40mg magnesium, 450mg potassium.

SPICY GRILLED SHRIMP WITH AVOCADO SALSA

- 10 oz large shrimp, peeled and deveined
- 1 tbsp olive oil
- 1 tsp lime juice
- 1/2 tsp smoked paprika
- 1/2 tsp chili powder
- 1/4 tsp cumin
- 1/4 tsp black pepper
- 1/4 tsp garlic powder

For the Avocado Salsa:
- 1 medium avocado, diced
- 1/2 cup cherry tomatoes, diced
- 1/4 cup red onion, finely chopped
- 1 tbsp fresh cilantro, chopped
- 1 tbsp lime juice
- 1/2 tsp olive oil
- 1/4 tsp black pepper

Prep time: 15 min   **Cook time:** 10 min   **Serves:** 2

DIRECTIONS

In a bowl, combine shrimp, olive oil, lime juice, smoked paprika, chili powder, cumin, black pepper, garlic powder and toss to cover. Let it marinate for 10 minutes.

In another bowl, mix avocado, cherry tomatoes, red onion, cilantro, lime juice, olive oil, and black pepper. Stir gently and set aside.

Preheat a grill or grill pan over medium heat. Cook the shrimp for 2–3 minutes per side until opaque and slightly charred.

Divide the shrimp onto two plates and top with avocado salsa. Serve immediately.

NUTRITIONAL INFORMATION (PER SERVING)

320 calories, 35g protein, 15g carbohydrates, 16g fats, 6g fiber, 220mg cholesterol, 350mg sodium, 45mg magnesium, 600mg potassium.

HERB-CRUSTED BAKED COD

INGREDIENTS

- 4 cod fillets (5 oz each)
- 2 tbsp olive oil
- 1/2 cup whole wheat breadcrumbs (or almond flour for gluten-free)
- 1 tbsp fresh parsley, chopped
- 1 tsp dried oregano
- 1/2 tsp dried thyme
- 1/2 tsp garlic powder
- 1/2 tsp black pepper
- 1 tbsp lemon juice

Prep time: 10 min   **Cook time:** 15 min   **Serves:** 4

DIRECTIONS

Preheat to 400°F (200°C) and line a baking sheet with parchment paper.

In a bowl, mix breadcrumbs, parsley, oregano, thyme, garlic powder, black pepper, and 1 tbsp olive oil.

Brush the cod fillets with the remaining olive oil and press the herb mixture onto the top of each fillet.

Place cod on the baking sheet and bake for 12–15 minutes, or until the fish flakes easily with a fork.

Drizzle with lemon juice and serve with steamed vegetables or quinoa.

NUTRITIONAL INFORMATION (PER SERVING)

230 calories, 32g protein, 10g carbohydrates, 8g fats, 1g fiber, 65mg cholesterol, 180mg sodium, 45mg magnesium, 500mg potassium.

ZESTY LEMON AND GARLIC SHRIMP SKEWERS

INGREDIENTS

- 1 lb large shrimp, peeled and deveined
- 2 tbsp olive oil
- 2 tbsp lemon juice
- 2 garlic cloves, minced
- 1 tsp lemon zest
- 1/2 tsp black pepper
- 1/2 tsp paprika
- 1/4 tsp red pepper flakes (optional)
- 1 tbsp fresh parsley, chopped (for garnish)
- 4 wooden or metal skewers

Prep time: 5 min   **Serves:** 2

DIRECTIONS

Whisk olive oil, lemon juice, garlic, lemon zest, black pepper, paprika, and red pepper flakes (if using) in a bowl.

Toss shrimp in the marinade and refrigerate for 15 minutes.

Soak wooden skewers in water for 10 minutes if using, then thread shrimp onto skewers.

Preheat a grill over medium-high heat and cook shrimp for 2–3 min per side until pink.

Garnish with parsley and serve with quinoa, rice, or grilled veggies.

NUTRITIONAL INFORMATION (PER SERVING)

220 calories, 32g protein, 3g carbohydrates, 9g fats, 0g fiber, 200mg cholesterol, 250mg sodium, 45mg magnesium, 400mg potassium.

MUSTARD AND HERB BAKED SALMON PATTIES

INGREDIENTS

- 1 lb cooked salmon (or canned wild salmon, drained and flaked)
- 1/2 cup whole wheat breadcrumbs (or almond flour for gluten-free)
- 1 egg
- 2 tbsp Dijon mustard
- 1 tbsp olive oil
- 2 tbsp fresh parsley, chopped
- 1 tbsp fresh dill, chopped (or 1/2 tsp dried dill)
- 1/2 tsp garlic powder
- 1/2 tsp black pepper
- 1/4 tsp smoked paprika
- 1 tbsp lemon juice

Prep time: 10 min   **Cook time:** 20 min   **Serves:** 4 (8 patties)

DIRECTIONS

Preheat to 400°F (200°C) and line a baking sheet with parchment paper.

In a bowl, mix flaked salmon, breadcrumbs, egg, Dijon mustard, olive oil, parsley, dill, garlic powder, black pepper, smoked paprika, and lemon juice until well combined.

Shape the mixture into 8 small patties and place them on the baking sheet.

Bake for 18–20 minutes, flipping halfway through, until golden brown and firm.

Let cool for a few min and serve with a side of mixed greens or a yogurt-based dip.

NUTRITIONAL INFORMATION (PER SERVING - 2 PATTIES)

280 calories, 32g protein, 10g carbohydrates, 13g fats, 1g fiber, 80mg cholesterol, 250mg sodium, 50mg magnesium, 500mg potassium.

BERRY BANANA SMOOTHIE

INGREDIENTS

- 1 banana
- 1 cup mixed berries (fresh or frozen)
- 1 cup unsweetened almond milk
- 1 tbsp flaxseeds
- 1 tsp honey (optional)

Prep time: 5 min   **Serves:** 2

DIRECTIONS

Combine all ingredients in a blender.

Blend until smooth.

NUTRITIONAL INFORMATION (PER SERVING)

150 calories, 3g protein, 30g carbohydrates, 3g fats, 7g fiber, 0mg cholesterol, 50mg sodium, 40mg magnesium, 400mg potassium.

SMOOTHIE BOWL WITH SPINACH AND BERRIES

INGREDIENTS

- 1 cup spinach leaves
- 1 cup mixed berries (blueberries, strawberries, raspberries)
- 1 banana
- 1/2 cup Greek yogurt (low-fat or fat-free)
- 1/2 cup almond milk (unsweetened)
- 1 tbsp chia seeds (optional)
- 1 tbsp honey (optional)

Prep time: 10 min   **Serves:** 2

DIRECTIONS

Divide the muesli evenly between two bowls.

Pour 1/2 cup of almond milk over the muesli in each bowl. Stir gently to combine.

Add the fresh mixed fruit evenly over the top of each bowl.

Sprinkle chia seeds or flaxseeds on top for extra nutrients, and drizzle with honey or maple syrup if desired.

NUTRITIONAL INFORMATION (PER SERVING)

150 calories, 3g protein, 30g carbohydrates, 3g fats, 7g fiber, 0mg cholesterol, 50mg sodium, 40mg magnesium, 400mg potassium.

HEART-HEALTHY APPLE AND BANANA SMOOTHIE

INGREDIENTS

- 1 medium apple (cored and chopped)
- 1 medium banana (peeled and sliced)
- 1 cup unsweetened almond milk (or low-fat milk)
- 1/2 cup Greek yogurt (plain, unsweetened)
- 1/2 tsp cinnamon
- 1 tsp chia seeds (optional)
- 1/2 tsp vanilla extract
- 1/2 cup ice cubes (optional)

Prep time: 5 min   **Serves:** 2

DIRECTIONS

Wash, core, and chop the apple. Peel and slice the banana.

In a blender, combine the apple, banana, almond milk, Greek yogurt, cinnamon, vanilla extract, and chia seeds (if using). Add ice cubes for a chilled smoothie.

Process on high speed for 30-60 seconds until creamy.

Pour into glasses and enjoy immediately.

NUTRITIONAL INFORMATION (PER SERVING)

160 calories, 6g protein, 30g carbohydrates, 3g fats, 5g fiber, 3mg cholesterol, 50mg sodium, 50mg magnesium, 450mg potassium.

SMOOTHIE BOWL WITH FLAXSEEDS AND BLUEBERRIES

INGREDIENTS

- 1 cup frozen blueberries
- 1 frozen banana
- 1 cup unsweetened almond milk (or any plant-based milk)
- 2 tbsp ground flaxseeds
- 1/2 cup plain unsweetened Greek yogurt (optional, for added creaminess)
- 1/2 cup fresh blueberries (for topping)
- 2 tbsp granola (for topping)
- 2 tsp chia seeds (optional, for topping)

Prep time: 5 min   **Serves:** 2

DIRECTIONS

In a blender, combine the frozen blueberries, frozen banana, almond milk, ground flaxseeds, and Greek yogurt (if using). Blend until smooth and creamy.

Pour the smoothie mixture into a bowl. Arrange fresh blueberries, granola, and chia seeds (if using) on top.

Serve immediately as a refreshing, nutrient-packed breakfast or snack.

NUTRITIONAL INFORMATION (PER SERVING)

250 calories, 6g protein, 37g carbohydrates, 8g fats, 8g fiber, 0mg cholesterol, 50mg sodium, 60mg magnesium, 400mg potassium.

CHOCOLATE AVOCADO SMOOTHIE

INGREDIENTS

- 1 ripe avocado
- 1 medium banana, frozen
- 2 tbsp unsweetened cocoa powder
- 1 cup unsweetened almond milk (or any plant-based milk)
- 1 tbsp honey or maple syrup (optional, for sweetness)
- 1/2 tsp vanilla extract
- 4–5 ice cubes (optional, for a chilled smoothie)

Prep time: 5 min   **Serves:** 2

DIRECTIONS

Scoop the flesh from the avocado and peel the frozen banana.

In a blender, combine the avocado, frozen banana, cocoa powder, almond milk, honey or maple syrup (if using), vanilla extract, and ice cubes.

Blend on high speed for 1–2 minutes, or until the smoothie is creamy and well combined.

Divide the smoothie evenly between two glasses and serve immediately.

NUTRITIONAL INFORMATION (PER SERVING)

220 calories, 5g protein, 22g carbohydrates, 14g fats, 7g fiber, 0mg cholesterol, 60mg sodium, 60mg magnesium, 500mg potassium.

GREEN APPLE AND KALE SMOOTHIE

INGREDIENTS

- 1 medium green apple, cored and sliced
- 1 cup fresh kale leaves (packed, stems removed)
- 1/2 cucumber, peeled and sliced
- 1 cup unsweetened almond milk (or water)
- 1 tbsp lemon juice
- 1/2 tsp grated fresh ginger (optional)
- 1 tsp chia seeds or flaxseeds (optional, for added fiber)
- 4–5 ice cubes (optional, for a chilled smoothie)

Prep time: 5 min   **Serves:** 2

DIRECTIONS

Core and slice the green apple, and remove the stems from the kale leaves. Peel and slice the cucumber.

Add the green apple, kale, cucumber, almond milk, lemon juice, ginger (if using), chia seeds or flaxseeds (if using), and ice cubes to a blender.

Blend on high speed for 1–2 minutes, or until the mixture is smooth and creamy.

Divide the smoothie evenly between two glasses and serve immediately.

NUTRITIONAL INFORMATION (PER SERVING)

120 calories, 3g protein, 22g carbohydrates, 3g fats, 5g fiber, 0mg cholesterol, 40mg sodium, 40mg magnesium, 300mg potassium.

STRAWBERRY KIWI SMOOTHIE

INGREDIENTS

- 1 cup fresh or frozen strawberries
- 2 ripe kiwis, peeled and sliced
- 1/2 cup plain unsweetened Greek yogurt
- 1/2 cup unsweetened almond milk (or any plant-based milk)
- 1 tsp honey or maple syrup (optional, for sweetness)
- 4–5 ice cubes (optional, for a chilled smoothie)

Prep time: 5 min   **Serves:** 2

DIRECTIONS

Wash the strawberries, peel, and slice the kiwis.

In a blender, combine the strawberries, kiwis, Greek yogurt, almond milk, honey or maple syrup (if using), and ice cubes.

Blend on high speed for 1–2 minutes, or until the mixture is smooth and creamy.

Divide the smoothie evenly between two glasses and serve immediately.

NUTRITIONAL INFORMATION (PER SERVING)

130 calories, 5g protein, 22g carbohydrates, 2g fats, 4g fiber, 5mg cholesterol, 40mg sodium, 25mg magnesium, 300mg potassium.

PEANUT BUTTER AND BANANA SMOOTHIE

INGREDIENTS

- 1 large ripe banana, frozen
- 2 tbsp natural peanut butter
- 1 cup unsweetened almond or other plant-based milk
- 1/4 cup plain unsweetened Greek yogurt (optional, for added creaminess)
- 1/2 tsp vanilla extract
- 1 tsp honey, date, or maple syrup (optional)
- 4–5 ice cubes (optional, for a chilled smoothie)

Prep time: 5 min   **Serves:** 2

DIRECTIONS

Peel the frozen banana and slice it into chunks.

In a blender, combine the banana, peanut butter, almond milk, Greek yogurt (if using), vanilla extract, honey or maple syrup (if using), and ice cubes.

Blend on high speed for 1–2 minutes, or until the smoothie is creamy and smooth.

NUTRITIONAL INFORMATION (PER SERVING)

200 calories, 7g protein, 22g carbohydrates, 9g fats, 3g fiber, 0mg cholesterol, 60mg sodium, 50mg magnesium, 400mg potassium.

OATMEAL BERRY BREAKFAST SMOOTHIE

INGREDIENTS

- 1/2 cup rolled oats (gluten-free certified if needed)
- 1 cup frozen mixed berries (blueberries, strawberries, raspberries)
- 1 medium banana, sliced
- 1 cup unsweetened almond or any plant-based milk
- 1/4 cup plain unsweetened Greek yogurt (optional, for added creaminess)
- 1 tbsp chia seeds (optional, for added fiber)
- 1/2 tsp vanilla extract
- 1 tsp honey, date, or maple syrup (optional)

Prep time: 5 min   **Serves:** 2

DIRECTIONS

Add the rolled oats, frozen berries, banana, almond milk, Greek yogurt (if using), chia seeds, vanilla extract, and honey or maple syrup (if using) to a blender.

Blend on high speed for 1–2 minutes, or until the mixture is creamy and smooth.

NUTRITIONAL INFORMATION (PER SERVING)

210 calories, 6g protein, 36g carbohydrates, 4g fats, 6g fiber, 0mg cholesterol, 50mg sodium, 50mg magnesium, 300mg potassium.

AVOCADO SPINACH SMOOTHIE

INGREDIENTS

- 1/2 ripe avocado
- 1 cup fresh spinach leaves (packed)
- 1 medium banana, sliced
- 1 cup unsweetened almond or any plant-based milk
- 1/2 tsp vanilla extract
- 1 tsp honey, date, or maple syrup (optional)
- 4–5 ice cubes (optional, for a chilled smoothie)

Prep time: 5 min   **Serves:** 2

DIRECTIONS

Scoop out the flesh of the avocado, rinse the spinach leaves, and slice the banana.

Add the avocado, spinach, banana, almond milk, vanilla extract, honey or maple syrup (if using), and ice cubes to a blender.

Blend on high speed for 1–2 minutes, or until the smoothie is creamy and smooth.

NUTRITIONAL INFORMATION (PER SERVING)

180 calories, 4g protein, 20g carbohydrates, 10g fats, 5g fiber, 0mg cholesterol, 40mg sodium, 50mg magnesium, 400mg potassium.

BANANA AND CASHEW ICE CREAM

INGREDIENTS

- 4 ripe bananas, peeled and sliced
- 1/2 cup raw cashews, soaked in water for at least 4 hours
- 1/2 cup unsweetened almond milk (or any plant-based milk)
- 1 tsp vanilla extract
- 1 tbsp maple syrup or honey (optional)

Prep time: 5 min   **Freeze time:** 4 hours   **Serves:** 4

DIRECTIONS

Place the sliced bananas on a parchment-lined tray and freeze for at least 4 hours or until solid.

Drain and rinse the soaked cashews, then blend them with almond milk in a high-speed blender until smooth.

Add the frozen banana slices, vanilla extract, and maple syrup (if using) to the blender. Blend until creamy, stopping to scrape down the sides as needed.

Serve immediately for a soft-serve consistency, or transfer to a container and freeze for 1–2 hours for a firmer texture.

NUTRITIONAL INFORMATION (PER SERVING)

180 calories, 3g protein, 31g carbohydrates, 6g fat, 3g fiber, 0mg cholesterol, 15mg sodium, 50mg magnesium, 400mg potassium.

DATE CHOCOLATE BALLS

INGREDIENTS

- 1 cup Medjool dates, pitted
- 1/2 cup almond flour
- 2 tbsp cacao powder
- 1 tsp vanilla extract
- 1/4 cup unsweetened coconut flakes, for coating

Prep time: 10 min   **Chill time:** 20 min   **Serves:** 12 balls

DIRECTIONS

In a bowl lend the dates with an immersion blender until they form a sticky paste.

Add almond flour, cacao powder, and vanilla extract to the food processor. Blend until the mixture comes together and forms a dough.

Scoop out about 1 tablespoon of the mixture at a time and roll it into small balls using your hands.

Roll each ball in the coconut flakes to coat evenly.

Place the balls in an airtight container and chill in the refrigerator for at least 20 minutes before serving.

NUTRITIONAL INFORMATION (PER BALL)

90 calories, 2g protein, 11g carbohydrates, 4g fat, 2g fiber, 0mg cholesterol, 5mg sodium, 130mg potassium, 25mg magnesium.

DATE AND NUT ENERGY BITES

INGREDIENTS

- 1 cup pitted Medjool dates
- 1/2 cup almonds (or any nut of choice)
- 1/4 cup walnuts
- 1/4 cup shredded unsweetened coconut
- 1 tbsp chia seeds
- 1 tsp vanilla extract

Prep time: 10 min   **Serves:** 12 bites

DIRECTIONS

Add dates, almonds, walnuts, coconut, chia seeds, and vanilla extract to a food processor. Blend until the mixture forms a sticky dough.

Scoop out about 1 tablespoon of the mixture and roll into balls.

Place in the refrigerator for at least 30 minutes to firm up.

Store in an airtight container in the fridge for up to 1 week.

NUTRITIONAL INFORMATION (PER BITE)

90 calories, 2g protein, 10g carbohydrates, 5g fats, 2g fiber, 0mg cholesterol, 5mg sodium, 20mg magnesium, 80mg potassium.

WHOLE-GRAIN FRUIT CRISP

INGREDIENTS

- 4 cups mixed fruit (e.g., apples, peaches, or berries)
- 1 tbsp lemon juice
- 1/4 cup rolled oats
- 1/4 cup whole wheat flour
- 2 tbsp brown sugar or coconut sugar
- 2 tbsp unsalted butter or coconut oil, melted
- 1/2 tsp cinnamon

Prep time: 10 min   **Cook time:** 30 min   **Serves:** 6

DIRECTIONS

Preheat to 375°F (190°C).

Toss mixed fruit with lemon juice and place in a baking dish.

For topping combine oats, flour, sugar, butter, and cinnamon in a bowl until crumbly.

Sprinkle the topping evenly over the fruit. Bake for 30 min or until it becomes bubbly and golden.

Cool slightly and serve warm.

NUTRITIONAL INFORMATION (PER BITE)

160 calories, 3g protein, 28g carbohydrates, 5g fats, 4g fiber, 10mg cholesterol, 20mg sodium, 25mg magnesium, 200mg potassium.

COCONUT CHIA ENERGY BARS

INGREDIENTS

- 1 cup rolled oats
- 1/2 cup shredded unsweetened coconut
- 1/4 cup chia seeds
- 1/4 cup almond butter
- 1/4 cup honey or maple syrup
- 1 tsp vanilla extract

Prep time: 10 min   **Serves:** 8 bars

DIRECTIONS

Combine oats, coconut, chia seeds, almond butter, honey, and vanilla in a bowl until evenly mixed.

Press the mixture firmly into a parchment-lined 8x8-inch pan.

Refrigerate for at least 1 hour until firm.

Slice into 8 bars and store in the fridge for up to 1 week.

NUTRITIONAL INFORMATION (PER BAR)

190 calories, 5g protein, 20g carbohydrates, 10g fats, 5g fiber, 0mg cholesterol, 25mg sodium, 30mg magnesium, 150mg potassium.

QUINOA PUDDING

INGREDIENTS

- 1/2 cup quinoa, rinsed
- 1 1/2 cups unsweetened almond milk
- 2 tbsp honey or maple syrup
- 1 tsp vanilla extract
- 1/4 tsp cinnamon
- Optional: Fresh fruit for topping

Prep time: 5 min   **Cook time:** 20 min   **Serves:** 4

DIRECTIONS

In a pot, combine quinoa and almond milk and bring to a boil. Then reduce heat, and let it simmer for 15 min until tender.

Stir in honey, vanilla, and cinnamon. Simmer for 5 more min, stirring occasionally.

Divide into bowls and top with fresh fruit if desired.

NUTRITIONAL INFORMATION (PER SERVING)

160 calories, 5g protein, 25g carbohydrates, 4g fats, 3g fiber, 0mg cholesterol, 40mg sodium, 50mg magnesium, 150mg potassium.

PUMPKIN SPICE MUFFINS

INGREDIENTS

- 1 1/2 cups whole wheat flour
- 1/2 cup rolled oats
- 1 tsp baking powder
- 1 tsp cinnamon
- 1/2 tsp nutmeg
- 1/4 tsp ginger
- 1/4 tsp salt
- 1 cup pumpkin puree
- 1/2 cup maple syrup
- 2 eggs
- 1/4 cup coconut oil, melted

Prep time: 10 min   **Cook time:** 20 min   **Serves:** 12 muffins

DIRECTIONS

Preheat to 350°F (175°C) and line a muffin tin with liners.

Combine flour, oats, baking powder, cinnamon, nutmeg, ginger, and salt in a bowl.

In another bowl, whisk pumpkin puree, maple syrup, eggs, and coconut oil.

Mix wet and dry ingredients until just combined. Divide batter among muffin liners and bake for 20 min.

Let cool before serving.

NUTRITIONAL INFORMATION (PER MUFFIN)

140 calories, 3g protein, 20g carbohydrates, 6g fats, 3g fiber, 15mg cholesterol, 80mg sodium, 20mg magnesium, 100mg potassium.

PEACH AND RASPBERRY SORBET

INGREDIENTS

- 2 cups frozen peach slices
- 1 cup frozen raspberries
- 2 tbsp honey or maple syrup (optional, for sweetness)
- 1 tbsp lemon juice
- 1/4 cup water

Prep time: 5 min   **Freeze time:** 4 hours   **Serves:** 4

DIRECTIONS

Freeze peaches and raspberries.

Add peaches, raspberries, honey (if using), lemon juice, and water to a blender or food processor. Blend until smooth.

Transfer the mixture to an airtight container and freeze for at least 2 hours to firm up.

Scoop into bowls and serve immediately.

NUTRITIONAL INFORMATION (PER SERVING)

90 calories, 1g protein, 21g carbohydrates, 0.5g fats, 4g fiber, 0mg cholesterol, 5mg sodium, 15mg magnesium, 200mg potassium.

ZUCCHINI CHOCOLATE CAKE

INGREDIENTS

- 1 1/2 cups shredded zucchini
- 1 cup whole wheat flour
- 1/2 cup cocoa powder
- 1 tsp baking soda
- 1/2 cup maple syrup or honey
- 1/4 cup coconut oil, melted
- 1/2 cup unsweetened almond milk
- 1 tsp vanilla extract

Prep time: 15 min   **Cook time:** 35 min   **Serves:** 8

DIRECTIONS

Preheat to 400°F (200°C) and line a baking sheet with parchment paper.

In a bowl, mix breadcrumbs, parsley, oregano, thyme, garlic powder, black pepper, and 1 tbsp olive oil.

Brush the cod fillets with the remaining olive oil and press the herb mixture onto the top of each fillet.

Place cod on the baking sheet and bake for 12–15 minutes, or until the fish flakes easily with a fork.

Drizzle with lemon juice and serve with steamed vegetables or quinoa.

NUTRITIONAL INFORMATION (PER SERVING)

150 calories, 3g protein, 25g carbohydrates, 6g fats, 3g fiber, 0mg cholesterol, 325mg sodium, 20mg magnesium, 150mg potassium.

APPLE NACHOS

INGREDIENTS

- 1 large apple, thinly sliced
- 2 tbsp natural peanut butter or almond butter
- 1 tbsp honey (optional)
- 1 tbsp shredded unsweetened coconut
- 1 tbsp mini dark chocolate chips (optional)

Prep time: 5 min   **Serves:** 2

DIRECTIONS

Thinly slice the apple and arrange on a plate.

Warm the peanut butter slightly and drizzle over the apple slices. Add honey if using.

Sprinkle with coconut and chocolate chips.

Enjoy immediately as a quick and healthy dessert.

NUTRITIONAL INFORMATION (PER SERVING)

180 calories, 4g protein, 26g carbohydrates, 8g fats, 4g fiber, 0mg cholesterol, 60mg sodium, 20mg magnesium, 200mg potassium.

DARK CHOCOLATE AVOCADO BROWNIES

INGREDIENTS

- 1 ripe avocado, mashed
- 2 large eggs
- 1/2 cup coconut sugar or brown sugar
- 1/4 cup cocoa powder
- 1/2 cup dark chocolate chips, melted
- 1/4 cup almond flour
- 1/2 tsp baking powder

Prep time: 10 min   **Cook time:** 20 min   **Serves:** 8 brownies

DIRECTIONS

Preheat to 350°F (175°C) and line an 8x8-inch pan with parchment paper.

In a bowl, whisk mashed avocado, eggs, sugar, and melted chocolate until smooth.

Add cocoa powder, almond flour, and baking powder. Mix until just combined.

Pour the batter into the pan and bake for 18–20 min. Let cool before cutting.

Slice into 8 pieces and serve.

NUTRITIONAL INFORMATION (PER BROWNIE)

160 calories, 4g protein, 16g carbohydrates, 10g fats, 3g fiber, 35mg cholesterol, 60mg sodium, 20mg magnesium, 150mg potassium.

HEART-HEALTHY BLUEBERRY CHEESECAKE

INGREDIENTS

- 1 cup oat flour
- 1/4 cup ground almonds
- 2 tbsp coconut oil, melted
- 2 tbsp honey or maple syrup
- 1/2 tsp cinnamon

Filling:
- 1 1/2 cup low-fat cream cheese or Greek yogurt
- 1/4 cup honey or maple syrup
- 1 large egg
- 1 tsp vanilla extract
- 1 tsp lemon zest

Blueberry Topping:
- 1 cup fresh or frozen blueberries
- 1 tbsp honey
- 1 tsp cornstarch mixed with 1 tbsp water

Prep time: 5 min   **Serves:** 2

DIRECTIONS

Preheat oven to 325°F (160°C) and grease an 8-inch springform pan.

Mix oat flour, almonds, cinnamon, coconut oil, and honey, then press into the pan. Bake for 10 minutes and cool.

Blend cream cheese, honey, egg, vanilla, and lemon zest, then pour over crust and bake 30-35 minutes until set.

Cook blueberries with honey and cornstarch, cool, spread over cheesecake, and chill 2 hours before serving.

NUTRITIONAL INFORMATION (PER SERVING)

190 calories, 6g protein, 24g carbohydrates, 8g fats, 2g fiber, 25mg cholesterol, 95mg sodium, 20mg magnesium, 130mg potassium.

FLAXSEED BREAD WITH WALNUTS AND RAISINS

INGREDIENTS

- 1 cup ground flaxseeds (flaxseed meal)
- 1 cup unsweetened Greek yogurt
- 1 tbsp sesame seeds for topping
- 1/4 cup chopped walnuts
- 1/4 cup raisins
- 1/2 tsp gluten-free baking powder
- 1/2 tsp cinnamon
- 1 egg
- 1 tbsp olive oil

Prep time: 5 min   **Cook time:** 5 min   **Serves:** 1 small loaf (6 slices)

DIRECTIONS

Grease a microwave-safe loaf pan.

In a bowl, mix flaxseeds, baking powder, cinnamon, walnuts, and raisins.

In another bowl, beat the egg, then add yogurt and olive oil.

Combine wet and dry ingredients, mix into a thick batter, and let sit 1–2 minutes and pour into the pan, smooth, and sprinkle sesame seeds.

Bake at 350°F (175°C) for 30–35 minutes or microwave for 4–5 minutes until firm.

NUTRITIONAL INFORMATION (PER SERVING)

158 calories, 6.5g protein, 11g carbohydrates, 11g fat, 5g fiber, 24mg cholesterol, 47mg sodium, 197mg potassium, 64mg magnesium.

BUCKWHEAT BREAD

INGREDIENTS

- 2 cups raw buckwheat groats
- 1/2 cup water (for blending)
- 1/4 cup chia seeds
- 1/2 cup water (to soak chia seeds)
- 1 tsp gluten-free baking soda
- 1 tsp apple cider vinegar
- 1/4 cup sunflower seeds or pumpkin seeds (optional, for topping)

Prep time: 15 min   **Cook time:** 50 min   **Serves:** 10 slices

DIRECTIONS

Rinse buckwheat groats and soak for 4 hours or overnight, then drain and rinse.

Mix chia seeds with 1/2 cup water and let sit for 10–15 minutes until gel forms.

Blend buckwheat, chia gel, 1/2 cup water, baking soda, and vinegar until smooth.

Preheat oven to 350°F (175°C), line a loaf pan, pour batter, smooth, and top with seeds.

Bake for 50 min, cool completely, and slice into 10 pieces.

NUTRITIONAL INFORMATION (PER SERVING)

120 calories, 4g protein, 20g carbohydrates, 3g fats, 4g fiber, 0mg cholesterol, 10mg sodium, 40mg magnesium, 100mg potassium.

LENTIL BREAD

INGREDIENTS

- 1 1/2 cups red or yellow lentils (dry)
- 1/2 cup water (for blending)
- 1/4 cup chia seeds
- 1/2 cup water (to soak chia seeds)
- 1 tsp gluten-free baking powder
- 1 tsp apple cider vinegar
- 1/4 tsp garlic powder (optional, for flavor)
- 1/4 tsp cumin powder (optional, for flavor)
- 1/4 cup sesame seeds or sunflower seeds (optional, for topping)

Prep time: 10 min **Cook time:** 45 min **Serves:** 10 slices

DIRECTIONS

Rinse lentils and soak for 4 hours or overnight, then drain and rinse. Mix chia seeds with 1/2 cup water and let sit for 10–15 minutes until gel forms.

Blend lentils, chia gel, 1/2 cup water, baking powder, vinegar, garlic powder, and cumin until smooth.

Preheat oven to 375°F (190°C), line a loaf pan, pour batter, smooth, and top with seeds.

Bake for 40–45 minutes, cool completely, and slice into 10 pieces.

NUTRITIONAL INFORMATION (PER SERVING)

130 calories, 7g protein, 18g carbohydrates, 2g fats, 4g fiber, 0mg cholesterol, 40mg sodium, 25mg magnesium, 150mg potassium.

ALMOND FLOUR BREAD

INGREDIENTS

- 2 cups almond flour
- 1/4 cup ground flaxseed
- 1 tsp baking powder (gluten-free certified)
- 1/4 tsp salt (optional)
- 3 large eggs
- 1/4 cup unsweetened almond milk
- 1 tbsp apple cider vinegar
- 1 tbsp olive oil or melted coconut oil

Prep time: 10 min **Cook time:** 40 min **Serves:** 12 slices

DIRECTIONS

Preheat oven to 350°F (175°C) and line a loaf pan.

In a bowl, whisk almond flour, flaxseed, baking powder, and salt.

In another bowl, whisk eggs, almond milk, vinegar, and olive oil.

Gradually mix wet and dry ingredients until a thick batter forms.

Pour into the pan, smooth the top, and bake for 35–40 minutes.

Cool completely before slicing into 12 pieces.

NUTRITIONAL INFORMATION (PER SERVING)

150 calories, 6g protein, 3g carbohydrates, 12g fats, 2g fiber, 55mg cholesterol, 50mg sodium, 40mg magnesium, 80mg potassium.

QUINOA AND FLAXSEED BREAD

INGREDIENTS

- 1 cup cooked quinoa (or 1/2 cup raw quinoa, cooked and cooled)
- 1/2 cup ground flaxseeds
- 1 cup almond flour
- 1/4 cup sunflower seeds (optional, for topping)
- 1 tsp baking powder (gluten-free certified)
- 1/2 tsp salt (optional)
- 3 large eggs
- 1/4 cup unsweetened almond milk
- 1 tbsp olive oil or melted coconut oil
- 1 tsp apple cider vinegar

Prep time: 10 min   **Cook time:** 45 min   **Serves:** 12 slices

DIRECTIONS

Preheat oven to 350°F (175°C) and line a loaf pan.
In a bowl, whisk almond flour, flaxseeds, baking powder, salt, and cooked quinoa.

In another bowl, whisk eggs, almond milk, olive oil, and vinegar.

Gradually mix wet and dry ingredients until a thick batter forms.

Pour into the pan, smooth, and sprinkle sunflower seeds if desired. Bake for 40–45 minutes, cool, and slice into 12 pieces.

NUTRITIONAL INFORMATION (PER SERVING)

180 calories, 6g protein, 9g carbohydrates, 13g fats, 3g fiber, 55mg cholesterol, 30mg sodium, 50mg magnesium, 100mg potassium.

SWEET POTATO OAT BREAD

INGREDIENTS

- 1 cup mashed sweet potato (cooked and cooled)
- 1 1/2 cups gluten-free certified oats, ground into flour
- 1/2 cup rolled oats (gluten-free certified, for texture)
- 1 tsp baking powder (gluten-free certified)
- 1/2 tsp cinnamon
- 1/4 tsp nutmeg (optional)
- 2 large eggs
- 1/4 cup unsweetened almond milk
- 2 tbsp olive oil
- 2 tbsp maple syrup or honey
- 1/4 tsp salt (optional)

Prep time: 5 min   **Cook time:** 50 min   **Serves:** 10 slices

DIRECTIONS

Preheat oven to 350°F (175°C) and line a loaf pan.

In a bowl, mix oat flour, oats, baking powder, cinnamon, nutmeg, and salt.

In another bowl, whisk mashed sweet potato, eggs, almond milk, olive oil, and maple syrup until smooth.

Gradually fold wet ingredients into dry without overmixing.

Pour batter into pan, smooth the top, and bake for 45–50 minutes.

Cool completely before slicing into 10 pieces.

NUTRITIONAL INFORMATION (PER SERVING)

150 calories, 4g protein, 23g carbohydrates, 5g fats, 3g fiber, 35mg cholesterol, 22mg sodium, 25mg magnesium, 150mg potassium.

WEEK 1 MEAL PLAN

Day	Breakfast	Lunch	Dinner	Snack	Smoothie	Dessert
Day 1	Berry Chia Seed Pudding	Spiced Carrot and Ginger Soup	Honey Mustard Glazed Pork Tenderloin	Celery Sticks with Nut Butter	Oatmeal Berry Breakfast Smoothie	Pumpkin Spice Muffins
Day 2	Apple Cinnamon Baked Oatmeal	Arugula and Beet Salad	Slow-Cooked Mediterranean Chicken Stew	Roasted Red Pepper and Chickpea Dip	Berry Banana Smoothie	Date and Nut Energy Bites
Day 3	Spinach and Feta Omelette	Broccoli Salad	Herb-Crusted Baked Cod	Kale and Avocado Dip	Avocado Spinach Smoothie	Date and Nut Energy Bites
Day 4	Smoked Salmon on Whole Grain Bagel with Avocado	Hearty Vegetarian Minestrone Soup	Sesame Ginger Turkey Meatballs	Kale and Avocado Dip	Peanut Butter and Banana Smoothie	Quinoa Pudding
Day 5	Greek Yogurt Parfait with Granola and Nuts	Mediterranean Lentil Soup	Lean Beef and Vegetable Stir-Fry	Garlic and Lemon Roasted Broccoli	Smoothie Bowl with Flaxseeds and Blueberries	Date and Nut Energy Bites
Day 6	Vegetable, Sweet Potato, and Black Bean Breakfast Bowl	Mediterranean Lentil Soup	Lean Beef and Vegetable Stir-Fry	Honey-Glazed Carrots	Green Apple and Kale Smoothie	Quinoa Pudding
Day 7	Homemade Granola with Nuts and Seeds	Mediterranean Chickpea Salad	Coconut Lime Grilled Chicken Thighs	Honey-Glazed Carrots	Berry Banana Smoothie	Quinoa Pudding

WEEK 2 MEAL PLAN

Day	Breakfast	Lunch	Dinner	Snack	Smoothie	Dessert
Day 8	Quinoa Breakfast Porridge with Almonds and Cinnamon	Avocado and Tomato Salad	Herb-Crusted Baked Cod	Roasted Red Pepper and Chickpea Dip	Berry Banana Smoothie	Dates Chocolate Balls
Day 9	Whole Grain English Muffin with Peanut Butter	Lemon Chicken and Quinoa Soup	Herb-Crusted Baked Cod	Garlic and Lemon Roasted Broccoli	Avocado Spinach Smoothie	Quinoa Pudding
Day 10	Apple Cinnamon Baked Oatmeal	Cauliflower Tabouleh	Cumin and Lime Grilled Flank Steak	Roasted Red Pepper and Chickpea Dip	Peanut Butter and Banana Smoothie	Dates Chocolate Balls
Day 11	Greek Yogurt Parfait with Granola and Nuts	Hearty Vegetarian Minestrone Soup	Coconut Lime Grilled Chicker Thighs	Baked Mixed Vegetable Chips	Smoothie Bowl with Spinach and Berries	Dates Chocolate Balls
Day 12	Greek Yogurt Parfait with Granola and Nuts	Hearty Vegetarian Minestrone Soup	Garlic & Yogurt Braised Georgian Chkmeruli Chicken	Kale and Avocado Dip	Green Apple and Kale Smoothie	Coconut Chia Energy Bars
Day 13	Homemade Granola with Nuts and Seeds	Lemon Chicken and Quinoa Soup	Slow-Cooked Mediterranean Chicken Stew	Honey-Glazed Carrots	Avocado Spinach Smoothie	Pumpkin Spice Muffins
Day 14	Overnight Oats with Berries	Rainbow Veggie Salad	Mustard and Herb Baked Salmon Patties	Tomato and Olive Tapenade on Crackers	Smoothie Bowl with Spinach and Berries	Zucchini Chocolate Cake

Day	Breakfast	Lunch	Dinner	Snack	Smoothie	Dessert
Day 15	Greek Yogurt Parfait with Berries	Slow-Cooked Beef and Vegetable Soup	Zesty Lemon and Garlic Shrimp Skewers	Stuffed Cherry Tomatoes with Cottage Cheese	Smoothie Bowl with Flaxseeds and Blueberries	Pumpkin Spice Muffins
Day 16	Quinoa Breakfast Porridge with Almonds and Cinnamon	Spiced Carrot and Ginger Soup	Greek Yogurt Marinated Grilled Chicken	Homemade Granola Clusters	Smoothie Bowl with Spinach and Berries	Banana and Cashew Ice Cream
Day 17	Greek Yogurt Parfait with Berries	Zucchini Salad with Tahini Dressing	Turkey and Quinoa Meatloaf	Celery Sticks with Nut Butter	Peanut Butter and Banana Smoothie	Dates Chocolate Balls
Day 18	Mediterranean Veggie Omelette	Mediterranean Chickpea Salad	Salmon Baked with Garlic and Herbs	Sautéed Zucchini and Mushrooms	Chocolate Avocado Smoothie	Banana and Cashew Ice Cream
Day 19	Buckwheat Pancakes with Maple Syrup and Pecans	Cauliflower Tabouleh	Slow-Cooked Mediterranean Chicken Stew	Honey-Glazed Carrots	Berry Banana Smoothie	Apple Nachos
Day 20	Brown Rice or Quinoa Bowl Topped with Avocado, Vegetables and Hummus	Lemon Chicken and Quinoa Soup	Rosemary and Garlic Roast Chicken	Tomato and Olive Tapenade on Crackers	Smoothie Bowl with Flaxseeds and Blueberries	Banana and Cashew Ice Cream
Day 21	Homemade Granola with Nuts and Seeds	Mediterranean Lentil Soup	Slow-Cooked Mediterranean Chicken Stew	Honey-Glazed Carrots	Chocolate Avocado Smoothie	Whole-Grain Fruit Crisp

WEEK 4 MEAL PLAN

Day	Breakfast	Lunch	Dinner	Snack	Smoothie	Dessert
Day 22	Whole Grain English Muffin with Peanut Butter	Zucchini Salad with Tahini Dressing	Slow-Cooked Mediterranean Chicken Stew	Baked Mixed Vegetable Chips	Smoothie Bowl with Flaxseeds and Blueberries	Peach and Raspberry Sorbet
Day 23	Whole Grain English Muffin with Peanut Butter	Zucchini Noodle Salad	Turkey and Quinoa Meatloaf	Sautéed Zucchini and Mushrooms	Chocolate Avocado Smoothie	Date and Nut Energy Bites
Day 24	Spinach and Feta Omelette	Green Salad with Daikon Radish and Cucumber	Slow-Cooked Mediterranean Chicken Stew	Stuffed Cherry Tomatoes with Cottage Cheese	Oatmeal Berry Breakfast Smoothie	Dates Chocolate Balls
Day 25	White Frittata with Vegetables	Avocado and Tomato Salad	Garlic & Yogurt Braised Georgian Chkmeruli Chicken	Celery Sticks with Nut Butter	Chocolate Avocado Smoothie	Date and Nut Energy Bites
Day 26	Whole Grain Bread Toast with Guacamole	Beef and Barley Soup	Cumin and Lime Grilled Flank Steak	Baked Mixed Vegetable Chips	Chocolate Avocado Smoothie	Zucchini Chocolate Cake
Day 27	Whole Grain English Muffin with Peanut Butter	Lemon Chicken and Quinoa Soup	Rosemary and Garlic Roast Chicken	Sautéed Zucchini and Mushrooms	Green Apple and Kale Smoothie	Apple Nachos
Day 28	Mediterranean Veggie Omelette	Georgian Tomato and Cucumber Salad	Zesty Lemon and Garlic Shrimp Skewers	Sautéed Zucchini and Mushrooms	Avocado Spinach Smoothie	Dates Chocolate Balls

Day	Breakfast	Lunch	Dinner	Snack	Smoothie	Dessert
Day 29	Quinoa Breakfast Bowl	Asian Cabbage Salad	Salmon Baked with Garlic and Herbs	Roasted Red Pepper and Chickpea Dip	Green Apple and Kale Smoothie	Dark Chocolate Avocado Brownies
Day 30	Smoked Salmon on Whole Grain Bagel with Avocado	Mediterranean Lentil Soup	Sesame Ginger Turkey Meatballs	Sautéed Zucchini and Mushrooms	Chocolate Avocado Smoothie	Coconut Chia Energy Bars
Day 31	Buckwheat Pancakes with Maple Syrup and Pecans	Rainbow Veggie Salad	Mustard and Herb Baked Salmon Patties	Roasted Red Pepper and Chickpea Dip	Chocolate Avocado Smoothie	Peach and Raspberry Sorbet
Day 32	Spinach and Feta Omelette	Hearty Vegetarian Minestrone Soup	Zesty Lemon and Garlic Shrimp Skewers	Baked Mixed Vegetable Chips	Avocado Spinach Smoothie	Peach and Raspberry Sorbet
Day 33	Greek Yogurt Parfait with Berries	Green Salad with Daikon Radish and Cucumber	Lean Beef and Vegetable Stir-Fry	Tomato and Olive Tapenade on Crackers	Smoothie Bowl with Flaxseeds and Blueberries	Quinoa Pudding
Day 34	Tofu Scramble with Vegetables	Mediterranean Chickpea Salad	Spicy Grilled Shrimp with Avocado Salsa	Celery Sticks with Nut Butter	Strawberry Kiwi Smoothie	Pumpkin Spice Muffins
Day 35	Berry Chia Seed Pudding	Cucumber and Dill Salad	Cumin and Lime Grilled Flank Steak	Roasted Red Pepper and Chickpea Dip	Oatmeal Berry Breakfast Smoothie	Apple Nachos

Day	Breakfast	Lunch	Dinner	Snack	Smoothie	Dessert
Day 36	Brown Rice or Quinoa Bowl Topped with Avocado, Vegetables and Hummus	Arugula and Beet Salad	Garlic & Yogurt Braised Georgian Chkmeruli Chicken	Roasted Red Pepper and Chickpea Dip	Avocado Spinach Smoothie	Quinoa Pudding
Day 37	Greek Yogurt Parfait with Berries	Slow-Cooked Beef and Vegetable Soup	Coconut Lime Grilled Chicken Thighs	Honey-Glazed Carrots	Smoothie Bowl with Spinach and Berries	Banana and Cashew Ice Cream
Day 38	Smoked Salmon on Whole Grain Bagel with Avocado	Avocado and Tomato Salad	Balsamic Glazed Turkey Breast	Garlic and Lemon Roasted Broccoli	Green Apple and Kale Smoothie	Apple Nachos
Day 39	Overnight Oats with Berries	Salmon and Avocado Salad	Spiced Lentil and Ground Turkey Skillet	Baked Mixed Vegetable Chips	Smoothie Bowl with Flaxseeds and Blueberries	Whole-Grain Fruit Crisp
Day 40	Brown Rice or Quinoa Bowl Topped with Avocado, Vegetables and Hummus	Hearty Vegetarian Minestrone Soup	Teriyaki Glazed Chicken Lettuce Wraps	Garlic and Lemon Roasted Broccoli	Oatmeal Berry Breakfast Smoothie	Coconut Chia Energy Bars
Day 41	Berry Chia Seed Pudding	Georgian Tomato and Cucumber Salad	Zesty Lemon and Garlic Shrimp Skewers	Garlic and Lemon Roasted Broccoli	Green Apple and Kale Smoothie	Dates Chocolate Balls
Day 42	Muesli with Almond Milk and Fresh Fruit	Mediterranean Lentil Soup	Rosemary and Garlic Roast Chicken	Honey-Glazed Carrots	Berry Banana Smoothie	Apple Nachos

Day	Breakfast	Lunch	Dinner	Snack	Smoothie	Dessert
Day 43	Whole Grain Bread Toast with Guacamole	Zucchini Noodle Salad	Balsamic Glazed Turkey Breast	Honey-Glazed Carrots	Smoothie Bowl with Spinach and Berries	Dates Chocolate Balls
Day 44	Apple Cinnamon Baked Oatmeal	Avocado and Tomato Salad	Mustard and Herb Baked Salmon Patties	Homemade Granola Clusters	Avocado Spinach Smoothie	Coconut Chia Energy Bars
Day 45	Smoked Salmon on Whole Grain Bagel with Avocado	Avocado and Tomato Salad	Cumin and Lime Grilled Flank Steak	Tomato and Olive Tapenade on Crackers	Strawberry Kiwi Smoothie	Dark Chocolate Avocado Brownies
Day 46	Whole Grain Pancakes	Broccoli Salad	Teriyaki Glazed Chicken Lettuce Wraps	Stuffed Cherry Tomatoes with Cottage Cheese	Strawberry Kiwi Smoothie	Dates Chocolate Balls
Day 47	Smoked Salmon on Whole Grain Bagel with Avocado	Avocado and Tomato Salad	Herb-Crusted Baked Cod	Kale and Avocado Dip	Strawberry Kiwi Smoothie	Apple Nachos
Day 48	Muesli with Almond Milk and Fresh Fruit	Broccoli Salad	Spiced Lentil and Ground Turkey Skillet	Roasted Red Pepper and Chickpea Dip	Avocado Spinach Smoothie	Whole-Grain Fruit Crisp
Day 49	Tofu Scramble with Vegetables	Chickpea and Kale Soup	Balsamic Glazed Turkey Breast	Honey-Glazed Carrots	Strawberry Kiwi Smoothie	Apple Nachos

CONCLUSION

Eating heart-healthy doesn't have to be complicated or restrictive — it's about making mindful choices, enjoying wholesome ingredients, and embracing the joy of cooking. Through the recipes in this cookbook, you've discovered how simple, flavorful, and nourishing heart-friendly meals can be. Whether you're preparing a quick breakfast, a satisfying dinner, or a nutritious snack, each dish is designed to support your heart health while keeping your taste buds happy.

I hope this cookbook has inspired you to explore new flavors, experiment in the kitchen, and build lifelong healthy habits. Remember, small, consistent changes in your diet can lead to big improvements in your overall well-being. Thank you for allowing me to be part of your journey — I wish you happiness, health, and many delicious heart-healthy meals ahead!

With gratitude and good health,

Genny Green

IMPERIAL TO METRIC CONVERSION TABLE FOR RECIPES

Imperial	Metric
Weight	
1 ounce (oz)	28 grams (g)
4 ounces (oz)	113 grams (g)
8 ounces (oz)	227 grams (g)
1 pound (lb)	454 grams (g)
Volume (Liquids & Dry)	
1 teaspoon (tsp)	5 milliliters (ml)
1 tablespoon (tbsp)	15 milliliters (ml)
1 fluid ounce (fl oz)	30 milliliters (ml)
1/4 cup	60 milliliters (ml)
1/2 cup	120 milliliters (ml)
1 cup	240 milliliters (ml)
1 pint (pt)	473 milliliters (ml)
1 quart (qt)	946 milliliters (ml)
1 gallon (gal)	3.79 liters (L)
Temperature	
212°F	100°C (Boiling point)
400°F	204°C
375°F	190°C
350°F	177°C
325°F	163°C

B

banana
QUINOA BREAKFAST BOWL, 28
QUINOA BREAKFAST PORRIDGE WITH ALMONDS AND CINNAMON, 30
WHOLE GRAIN ENGLISH MUFFIN WITH PEANUT BUTTER, 31
CHOCOLATE AVOCADO SMOOTHIE, 74
BERRY BANANA SMOOTHIE, 72
SMOOTHIE BOWL WITH SPINACH AND BERRIES, 72
HEART-HEALTHY APPLE AND BANANA SMOOTHIE, 73
SMOOTHIE BOWL WITH FLAXSEEDS AND BLUEBERRIES, 73
PEANUT BUTTER AND BANANA SMOOTHIE, 75
OATMEAL BERRY BREAKFAST SMOOTHIE, 76
AVOCADO SPINACH SMOOTHIE, 76
BANANA AND CASHEW ICE CREAM, 77

basil
VEGETABLE STUFFED ZUCCHINI BOATS, 60

beef broth
BEEF AND BARLEY SOUP (LEAN BEEF), 50
SLOW-COOKED BEEF AND VEGETABLE SOUP, 51

beet
BAKED MIXED VEGETABLE CHIPS, 36
ARUGULA AND BEET SALAD, 48

bell peppers
TERIYAKI GLAZED CHICKEN LETTUCE WRAPS, 68
VEGAN LENTIL SLOPPY JOES, 60
SLOW-COOKED MEDITERRANEAN CHICKEN STEW, 62
LEAN BEEF AND VEGETABLE STIR-FRY, 63
MEDITERRANEAN VEGGIE OMELETTE, 28
WHITE FRITTATA WITH VEGETABLES, 29
VEGETABLE, SWEET POTATO, AND BLACK BEAN BREAKFAST BOWL, 30
TOFU SCRAMBLE WITH VEGETABLES, 32
RAINBOW VEGGIE SALAD, 42
VEGETABLE STIR-FRY WITH BROWN RICE, 55

WHOLE-WHEAT VEGGIE PIZZA, 56
STUFFED BELL PEPPERS, 58
THAI PEANUT NOODLES, 61

berries
OVERNIGHT OATS WITH BERRIES, 25
GREEK YOGURT PARFAIT WITH GRANOLA AND NUTS, 26
QUINOA BREAKFAST BOWL, 28
GREEK YOGURT PARFAIT WITH BERRIES, 29
QUINOA BREAKFAST PORRIDGE WITH ALMONDS AND CINNAMON, 30
BERRY CHIA SEED PUDDING, 33
BERRY BANANA SMOOTHIE, 72
SMOOTHIE BOWL WITH SPINACH AND BERRIES, 72
OATMEAL BERRY BREAKFAST SMOOTHIE, 76

black beans
STUFFED BELL PEPPERS, 58
VEGETABLE, SWEET POTATO, AND BLACK BEAN BREAKFAST BOWL, 30

black olives
WHOLE-WHEAT VEGGIE PIZZA, 56

black sesame seeds
GREEN SALAD WITH DAIKON RADISH AND CUCUMBER, 43

blueberries
SMOOTHIE BOWL WITH FLAXSEEDS AND BLUEBERRIES, 73
SMOOTHIE BOWL WITH FLAXSEEDS AND BLUEBERRIES, 73
HEART-HEALTHY BLUEBERRY CHEESECAKE, 82

broccoli
GARLIC AND LEMON ROASTED BROCCOLI, 39
BROCCOLI SALAD, 44
VEGETABLE STIR-FRY WITH BROWN RICE, 55
ROASTED VEGETABLE AND CHICKPEA SALAD, 59

LEAN BEEF AND VEGETABLE STIR-FRY, 63

brown rice
BROWN RICE OR QUINOA BOWL WITH AVOCADO, VEGETABLES, AND HUMMUS, 32
VEGETABLE STIR-FRY WITH BROWN RICE, 55

buckwheat
BUCKWHEAT BREAD, 83

buckwheat flour
BUCKWHEAT PANCAKES WITH MAPLE SYRUP AND PECANS, 35

butter
WHOLE-GRAIN FRUIT CRISP, 78

C

canned black beans
QUINOA AND BLACK BEAN BOWL, 53

canned chickpeas
ROASTED RED PEPPER AND CHICKPEA DIP, 39
CHICKPEA AND KALE VEGETARIAN SOUP, 51

canned kidney beans
HEARTY VEGETARIAN MINESTRONE SOUP, 52

canned tomatoes
MEDITERRANEAN LENTIL SOUP (VEGETARIAN), 49
BEEF AND BARLEY SOUP (LEAN BEEF), 50
SLOW-COOKED BEEF AND VEGETABLE SOUP, 51
HEARTY VEGETARIAN MINESTRONE SOUP, 52
LENTIL AND SPINACH CURRY, 53
CHICKPEA AND SPINACH MIDDLE EAST SHAKSHUKA, 57
SLOW-COOKED MEDITERRANEAN CHICKEN STEW, 62

capers
TOMATO AND OLIVE TAPENADE ON CRACKERS, 38

carrot
BROWN RICE OR QUINOA BOWL WITH AVOCADO, VEGETABLES, AND HUMMUS, 32
BAKED MIXED VEGETABLE CHIPS, 36
HONEY-GLAZED CARROTS, 40
RAINBOW VEGGIE SALAD, 42
ASIAN CABBAGE SALAD, 45
MEDITERRANEAN LENTIL SOUP (VEGETARIAN), 49
CHICKEN AND WILD RICE SOUP, 49
BEEF AND BARLEY SOUP (LEAN BEEF), 50
SLOW-COOKED BEEF AND VEGETABLE SOUP, 51
SLOW-COOKED BEEF AND VEGETABLE SOUP, 51
LEMON CHICKEN AND QUINOA SOUP, 52
HEARTY VEGETARIAN MINESTRONE SOUP, 52
VEGETABLE STIR-FRY WITH BROWN RICE, 55
CAULIFLOWER FRIED RICE, 57
THAI PEANUT NOODLES, 61
LEAN BEEF AND VEGETABLE STIR-FRY, 63
TURKEY AND QUINOA MEATLOAF, 63
TERIYAKI GLAZED CHICKEN LETTUCE WRAPS, 68

cashews
BANANA AND CASHEW ICE CREAM, 77

cauliflower
CAULIFLOWER TABOULEH, 41
CAULIFLOWER FRIED RICE, 57

celery
MEDITERRANEAN LENTIL SOUP (VEGETARIAN), 49
CHICKEN AND WILD RICE SOUP, 49
BEEF AND BARLEY SOUP (LEAN BEEF), 50
SLOW-COOKED BEEF AND VEGETABLE SOUP, 51
LEMON CHICKEN AND QUINOA SOUP, 52
HEARTY VEGETARIAN MINESTRONE SOUP, 52
CELERY STICKS WITH NUT BUTTER, 37

cherry tomatoes
WHOLE GRAIN BREAD TOAST WITH GUACAMOLE, 25
BROWN RICE OR QUINOA BOWL WITH AVOCADO, VEGETABLES, AND HUMMUS, 32

STUFFED CHERRY TOMATOES WITH COTTAGE CHEESE, 36
TOMATO AND OLIVE TAPENADE ON CRACKERS, 38
MEDITERRANEAN CHICKPEA SALAD, 41
RAINBOW VEGGIE SALAD, 42
ZUCCHINI NOODLE SALAD, 42
ZUCCHINI SALAD WITH TAHINI DRESSING, 47
SALMON AND AVOCADO SALAD, 48
QUINOA AND BLACK BEAN BOWL, 53
ROASTED VEGETABLE AND CHICKPEA SALAD, 59
SPICY GRILLED SHRIMP WITH AVOCADO SALSA, 69

chia seeds
OVERNIGHT OATS WITH BERRIES, 25
CHIA SEED PUDDING, 27
QUINOA BREAKFAST PORRIDGE WITH ALMONDS AND CINNAMON, 30
WHOLE GRAIN ENGLISH MUFFIN WITH PEANUT BUTTER, 31
BERRY CHIA SEED PUDDING, 33
MUESLI WITH ALMOND MILK AND FRESH FRUIT, 35
CELERY STICKS WITH NUT BUTTER, 37
HOMEMADE GRANOLA CLUSTERS, 37
SMOOTHIE BOWL WITH SPINACH AND BERRIES, 72
HEART-HEALTHY APPLE AND BANANA SMOOTHIE, 73
GREEN APPLE AND KALE SMOOTHIE, 74
DATE AND NUT ENERGY BITES, 78
COCONUT CHIA ENERGY BARS, 79
BUCKWHEAT BREAD, 83
LENTIL BREAD, 84
GREEK YOGURT PARFAIT WITH GRANOLA AND NUTS,26
QUINOA BREAKFAST BOWL, 28
SMOOTHIE BOWL WITH FLAXSEEDS AND BLUEBERRIES, 73
OATMEAL BERRY BREAKFAST SMOOTHIE, 76

chicken breast
CHICKEN AND WILD RICE SOUP, 49
LEMON CHICKEN AND QUINOA SOUP, 52
SLOW-COOKED MEDITERRANEAN CHICKEN STEW, 62

ROSEMARY AND GARLIC ROAST CHICKEN, 62
GREEK YOGURT MARINATED GRILLED CHICKEN, 65

chicken broth
CHICKEN AND WILD RICE SOUP, 49
LEMON CHICKEN AND QUINOA SOUP, 52
SLOW-COOKED MEDITERRANEAN CHICKEN STEW, 62
GARLIC & YOGURT BRAISED GEORGIAN CHKMERULI CHICKEN, 66
SPICED LENTIL AND GROUND TURKEY SKILLET, 67

chicken thighs
SLOW-COOKED MEDITERRANEAN CHICKEN STEW, 62
ROSEMARY AND GARLIC ROAST CHICKEN, 62
GARLIC & YOGURT BRAISED GEORGIAN CHKMERULI CHICKEN, 66
COCONUT LIME GRILLED CHICKEN THIGHS, 66

chickpeas
MEDITERRANEAN CHICKPEA SALAD, 41
EGGPLANT AND CHICKPEA STEW, 54
CHICKPEA AND SPINACH MIDDLE EAST SHAKSHUKA, 57
ROASTED VEGETABLE AND CHICKPEA SALAD, 59
SLOW-COOKED MEDITERRANEAN CHICKEN STEW, 62

chives
STUFFED CHERRY TOMATOES WITH COTTAGE CHEESE, 36

cilantro
WHOLE GRAIN BREAD TOAST WITH GUACAMOLE, 25
VEGETABLE, SWEET POTATO, AND BLACK BEAN BREAKFAST BOWL, 30
TOFU SCRAMBLE WITH VEGETABLES, 32
RAINBOW VEGGIE SALAD, 42
ASIAN CABBAGE SALAD, 45
AVOCADO AND TOMATO SALAD, 46
GEORGIAN EGGPLANT WITH WALNUTS, 46
QUINOA AND BLACK BEAN BOWL, 53
THAI PEANUT NOODLES, 61

CUMIN AND LIME GRILLED FLANK STEAK, 65
GARLIC & YOGURT BRAISED GEORGIAN CHKMERULI
CHICKEN, 66
COCONUT LIME GRILLED CHICKEN THIGHS, 66
SPICY GRILLED SHRIMP WITH AVOCADO SALSA, 69

cocoa powder
DATE CHOCOLATE BALLS, 77
CHOCOLATE AVOCADO SMOOTHIE, 74
ZUCCHINI CHOCOLATE CAKE, 81
DARK CHOCOLATE AVOCADO BROWNIES, 82

coconut flakes
DATE CHOCOLATE BALLS, 77

coconut milk
SPICED CARROT AND GINGER SOUP (VEGETARIAN)
LENTIL AND SPINACH CURRY, 53
COCONUT LIME GRILLED CHICKEN THIGHS, 66

coconut oil
HOMEMADE GRANOLA CLUSTERS, 37
WHOLE-GRAIN FRUIT CRISP, 78
PUMPKIN SPICE MUFFINS, 80
ZUCCHINI CHOCOLATE CAKE, 81
HEART-HEALTHY BLUEBERRY CHEESECAKE, 82
ALMOND FLOUR BREAD, 84
QUINOA AND FLAXSEED BREAD, 85

coconut sugar
WHOLE-GRAIN FRUIT CRISP, 78
DARK CHOCOLATE AVOCADO BROWNIES, 82

cod fillets
HERB-CRUSTED BAKED COD, 70

cooked salmon fillet
SALMON AND AVOCADO SALAD, 48

corn kernels
STUFFED BELL PEPPERS, 58

corn tortillas
TEMPEH TACOS, 58

cottage cheese
STUFFED CHERRY TOMATOES WITH COTTAGE
CHEESE, 36

cream cheese
ZUCCHINI NOODLE ALFREDO, 56
HEART-HEALTHY BLUEBERRY CHEESECAKE, 82

cucumber
BROWN RICE OR QUINOA BOWL WITH AVOCADO,
VEGETABLES, AND HUMMUS, 32
MEDITERRANEAN CHICKPEA SALAD, 41
CAULIFLOWER TABOULEH, 41
RAINBOW VEGGIE SALAD, 42
ZUCCHINI NOODLE SALAD, 42
CUCUMBER AND DILL SALAD, 43
GREEN SALAD WITH DAIKON RADISH AND
CUCUMBER, 43
GREEN APPLE AND KALE SMOOTHIE, 74

D
daikon radish
GREEN SALAD WITH DAIKON RADISH AND
CUCUMBER, 43

dark chocolate chips
APPLE NACHOS, 81
DARK CHOCOLATE AVOCADO BROWNIES, 82

dill
CUCUMBER AND DILL SALAD, 43
MUSTARD AND HERB BAKED SALMON PATTIES, 71

dried cranberries
BROCCOLI SALAD, 44

LEAN BEEF AND VEGETABLE STIR-FRY, 63
SESAME GINGER TURKEY MEATBALLS, 64
TERIYAKI GLAZED CHICKEN LETTUCE WRAPS, 68
PUMPKIN SPICE MUFFINS, 80

goat cheese
ARUGULA AND BEET SALAD, 48

granola
GREEK YOGURT PARFAIT WITH GRANOLA AND
NUTS,26
GREEK YOGURT PARFAIT WITH BERRIES, 29
SMOOTHIE BOWL WITH FLAXSEEDS AND
BLUEBERRIES, 73

Greek yogurt
GREEK YOGURT PARFAIT WITH GRANOLA AND
NUTS,26
GREEK YOGURT PARFAIT WITH BERRIES, 29
VEGETABLE, SWEET POTATO, AND BLACK BEAN
BREAKFAST BOWL, 30
KALE AND AVOCADO DIP, 38
BROCCOLI SALAD, 44
MUSHROOM STROGANOFF, 59
GREEK YOGURT MARINATED GRILLED CHICKEN, 65
GARLIC & YOGURT BRAISED GEORGIAN CHKMERULI
CHICKEN, 66
SMOOTHIE BOWL WITH SPINACH AND BERRIES, 72
HEART-HEALTHY APPLE AND BANANA SMOOTHIE, 73
SMOOTHIE BOWL WITH FLAXSEEDS AND
BLUEBERRIES, 73
STRAWBERRY KIWI SMOOTHIE, 75
PEANUT BUTTER AND BANANA SMOOTHIE, 75
OATMEAL BERRY BREAKFAST SMOOTHIE, 76
HEART-HEALTHY BLUEBERRY CHEESECAKE, 82
FLAXSEED BREAD WITH WALNUTS AND RAISINS, 83

green beans
SLOW-COOKED BEEF AND VEGETABLE SOUP, 51
HEARTY VEGETARIAN MINESTRONE SOUP, 52

green cabbage
ASIAN CABBAGE SALAD, 45

green onions
ASIAN CABBAGE SALAD, 45
CAULIFLOWER FRIED RICE, 57
THAI PEANUT NOODLES, 61
SESAME GINGER TURKEY MEATBALLS, 64
TERIYAKI GLAZED CHICKEN LETTUCE WRAPS, 68

ground almonds
HEART-HEALTHY BLUEBERRY CHEESECAKE, 82

ground chicken breast
TERIYAKI GLAZED CHICKEN LETTUCE WRAPS, 68

ground flaxseed
ALMOND FLOUR BREAD, 84
QUINOA AND FLAXSEED BREAD, 85

ground turkey
SPICED LENTIL AND GROUND TURKEY SKILLET, 67
TURKEY AND QUINOA MEATLOAF, 63
SESAME GINGER TURKEY MEATBALLS, 64

H
hummus
BROWN RICE OR QUINOA BOWL WITH AVOCADO,
VEGETABLES, AND HUMMUS, 32

K
Kalamata olives
TOMATO AND OLIVE TAPENADE ON CRACKERS, 38
MEDITERRANEAN CHICKPEA SALAD, 41
ZUCCHINI NOODLE SALAD, 42
SLOW-COOKED MEDITERRANEAN CHICKEN STEW, 62

kale
KALE AND AVOCADO DIP, 38
CHICKPEA AND KALE VEGETARIAN SOUP, 51
SWEET POTATO AND KALE STIR-FRY, 54

VEGAN LENTIL SLOPPY JOES, 60
SLOW-COOKED MEDITERRANEAN CHICKEN STEW, 62
TURKEY AND QUINOA MEATLOAF, 63
SPICED LENTIL AND GROUND TURKEY SKILLET, 67

P
Parmesan cheese
ZUCCHINI NOODLE ALFREDO, 56
STUFFED CHERRY TOMATOES WITH COTTAGE
CHEESE, 36

parsley
TOFU SCRAMBLE WITH VEGETABLES, 32
STUFFED CHERRY TOMATOES WITH COTTAGE
CHEESE, 36
TOMATO AND OLIVE TAPENADE ON CRACKERS, 38
SAUTÉED ZUCCHINI AND MUSHROOMS, 40
MEDITERRANEAN CHICKPEA SALAD, 41
CAULIFLOWER TABOULEH, 41
RAINBOW VEGGIE SALAD, 42
GREEN SALAD WITH DAIKON RADISH AND
CUCUMBER, 43
GEORGIAN TOMATO AND CUCUMBER SALAD, 46
ZUCCHINI SALAD WITH TAHINI DRESSING, 47
MEDITERRANEAN LENTIL SOUP (VEGETARIAN), 49
CHICKEN AND WILD RICE SOUP, 49
LEMON CHICKEN AND QUINOA SOUP, 52
EGGPLANT AND CHICKPEA STEW, 54
ZUCCHINI NOODLE ALFREDO, 56
MUSHROOM STROGANOFF, 59
SLOW-COOKED MEDITERRANEAN CHICKEN STEW, 62
GARLIC & YOGURT BRAISED GEORGIAN CHKMERULI
CHICKEN, 66
SPICED LENTIL AND GROUND TURKEY SKILLET, 67
SALMON BAKED WITH GARLIC AND HERBS, 69
HERB-CRUSTED BAKED COD, 70
ZESTY LEMON AND GARLIC SHRIMP SKEWERS, 70
MUSTARD AND HERB BAKED SALMON PATTIES, 71

parsnip
BAKED MIXED VEGETABLE CHIPS, 36

pasta
HEARTY VEGETARIAN MINESTRONE SOUP, 52
MUSHROOM STROGANOFF, 59

peach
PEACH AND RASPBERRY SORBET, 80

peanut butter
WHOLE GRAIN ENGLISH MUFFIN WITH PEANUT
BUTTER, 31
HOMEMADE GRANOLA CLUSTERS, 37
THAI PEANUT NOODLES, 61
PEANUT BUTTER AND BANANA SMOOTHIE, 75
APPLE NACHOS, 81

peanuts
ASIAN CABBAGE SALAD, 45

pearl barley
BEEF AND BARLEY SOUP (LEAN BEEF), 50

pecans
APPLE CINNAMON BAKED OATMEAL, 33
BUCKWHEAT PANCAKES WITH MAPLE SYRUP AND
PECANS, 35

pizza sauce
WHOLE-WHEAT VEGGIE PIZZA, 56

pomegranate seeds
GEORGIAN EGGPLANT WITH WALNUTS, 46

pork tenderloin
HONEY MUSTARD GLAZED PORK TENDERLOIN, 64

Portobello mushrooms
SPINACH AND FETA STUFFED PORTOBELLO
MUSHROOMS, 55

potato

SLOW-COOKED BEEF AND VEGETABLE SOUP, 51

pumpkin puree
PUMPKIN SPICE MUFFINS, 80

pumpkin seeds
RAINBOW VEGGIE SALAD, 42
BROWN RICE OR QUINOA BOWL WITH AVOCADO,
VEGETABLES, AND HUMMUS, 32
HOMEMADE GRANOLA WITH NUTS AND SEEDS, 34
BUCKWHEAT BREAD, 83

purple cabbage
RAINBOW VEGGIE SALAD, 42
ASIAN CABBAGE SALAD, 45

Q
quinoa
QUINOA BREAKFAST BOWL, 28
QUINOA BREAKFAST PORRIDGE WITH ALMONDS AND
CINNAMON, 30
BROWN RICE OR QUINOA BOWL WITH AVOCADO,
VEGETABLES, AND HUMMUS, 32
LEMON CHICKEN AND QUINOA SOUP, 52
QUINOA AND BLACK BEAN BOWL, 53
STUFFED BELL PEPPERS, 58
VEGETABLE STUFFED ZUCCHINI BOATS, 60
TURKEY AND QUINOA MEATLOAF, 63
QUINOA PUDDING, 79
QUINOA AND FLAXSEED BREAD, 85

R
raisins
FLAXSEED BREAD WITH WALNUTS AND RAISINS, 83

raspberries
PEACH AND RASPBERRY SORBET, 80

red onion
VEGETABLE, SWEET POTATO, AND BLACK BEAN
BREAKFAST BOWL, 30

MEDITERRANEAN CHICKPEA SALAD, 41
CAULIFLOWER TABOULEH, 41
RAINBOW VEGGIE SALAD, 42
ZUCCHINI NOODLE SALAD, 42
CUCUMBER AND DILL SALAD, 43
BROCCOLI SALAD, 44
AVOCADO AND TOMATO SALAD, 46
GEORGIAN TOMATO AND CUCUMBER SALAD, 46
ZUCCHINI SALAD WITH TAHINI DRESSING, 47
SALMON AND AVOCADO SALAD, 48
ARUGULA AND BEET SALAD, 48
SWEET POTATO AND KALE STIR-FRY, 54
SPICY GRILLED SHRIMP WITH AVOCADO SALSA, 69

roasted red peppers
ROASTED RED PEPPER AND CHICKPEA DIP, 39

rolled oats
OVERNIGHT OATS WITH BERRIES, 25
HOMEMADE GRANOLA CLUSTERS, 37
OATMEAL BERRY BREAKFAST SMOOTHIE, 76
WHOLE-GRAIN FRUIT CRISP, 78
COCONUT CHIA ENERGY BARS, 79
PUMPKIN SPICE MUFFINS, 80
SWEET POTATO OAT BREAD, 85

rosemary leaves
ROSEMARY AND GARLIC ROAST CHICKEN, 62

S
salad greens
SALMON AND AVOCADO SALAD, 48
ROASTED VEGETABLE AND CHICKPEA SALAD, 59

salmon
MUSTARD AND HERB BAKED SALMON PATTIES, 71
SALMON BAKED WITH GARLIC AND HERBS, 69

sesame oil
VEGETABLE STIR-FRY WITH BROWN RICE, 55
CAULIFLOWER FRIED RICE, 57

THAI PEANUT NOODLES, 61
SESAME GINGER TURKEY MEATBALLS, 64
TERIYAKI GLAZED CHICKEN LETTUCE WRAPS, 68

sesame seeds
ASIAN CABBAGE SALAD, 45
ZUCCHINI SALAD WITH TAHINI DRESSING, 47
SALMON AND AVOCADO SALAD, 48
THAI PEANUT NOODLES, 61
SESAME GINGER TURKEY MEATBALLS, 64
FLAXSEED BREAD WITH WALNUTS AND RAISINS, 83
LENTIL BREAD, 84
VEGETABLE STIR-FRY WITH BROWN RICE, 55
LEAN BEEF AND VEGETABLE STIR-FRY, 63
TERIYAKI GLAZED CHICKEN LETTUCE WRAPS, 68

shredded coconut
DATE AND NUT ENERGY BITES, 78
STUFFED BELL PEPPERS, 58
HOMEMADE GRANOLA WITH NUTS AND SEEDS, 34
HOMEMADE GRANOLA CLUSTERS, 37
COCONUT CHIA ENERGY BARS, 79
APPLE NACHOS, 81
BERRY CHIA SEED PUDDING, 33
CELERY STICKS WITH NUT BUTTER, 37

shrimp
SPICY GRILLED SHRIMP WITH AVOCADO SALSA, 69
ZESTY LEMON AND GARLIC SHRIMP SKEWERS, 70

smoked salmon
SMOKED SALMON ON WHOLE GRAIN BAGEL WITH AVOCADO, 34

snap peas
VEGETABLE STIR-FRY WITH BROWN RICE, 55
LEAN BEEF AND VEGETABLE STIR-FRY, 63

spaghetti
THAI PEANUT NOODLES, 61

spinach
SPINACH AND FETA OMELETTE, 26
MEDITERRANEAN VEGGIE OMELETTE, 28
WHITE FRITTATA WITH VEGETABLES, 29
VEGETABLE, SWEET POTATO, AND BLACK BEAN BREAKFAST BOWL, 30
SPINACH AND FETA BREAKFAST WRAP (WHOLE WHEAT), 31
TOFU SCRAMBLE WITH VEGETABLES, 32
LENTIL AND SPINACH CURRY, 53
SPINACH AND FETA STUFFED PORTOBELLO MUSHROOMS, 55
CHICKPEA AND SPINACH MIDDLE EAST SHAKSHUKA, 57
SPICED LENTIL AND GROUND TURKEY SKILLET, 67
SMOOTHIE BOWL WITH SPINACH AND BERRIES, 72
AVOCADO SPINACH SMOOTHIE, 76
WHOLE-WHEAT VEGGIE PIZZA, 56

strawberries
STRAWBERRY KIWI SMOOTHIE, 75

sunflower seeds
HOMEMADE GRANOLA WITH NUTS AND SEEDS, 34
RAINBOW VEGGIE SALAD, 42
BROCCOLI SALAD, 44
ZUCCHINI SALAD WITH TAHINI DRESSING, 47
SALMON AND AVOCADO SALAD, 48
BUCKWHEAT BREAD, 83
QUINOA AND FLAXSEED BREAD, 85
LENTIL BREAD, 84

sweet potato
VEGETABLE, SWEET POTATO, AND BLACK BEAN BREAKFAST BOWL, 30
ROASTED VEGETABLE AND CHICKPEA SALAD, 59
SWEET POTATO OAT BREAD, 85
SWEET POTATO AND KALE STIR-FRY, 54

T

tahini
ZUCCHINI SALAD WITH TAHINI DRESSING, 47

tempeh
TEMPEH TACOS, 58

tofu
TOFU SCRAMBLE WITH VEGETABLES, 32

tomato paste
VEGAN LENTIL SLOPPY JOES, 60
TURKEY AND QUINOA MEATLOAF, 63
TEMPEH TACOS, 58
VEGAN LENTIL SLOPPY JOES, 60

tomatoes
MEDITERRANEAN VEGGIE OMELETTE, 28
SMOKED SALMON ON WHOLE GRAIN BAGEL WITH AVOCADO, 34
CAULIFLOWER TABOULEH, 41
AVOCADO AND TOMATO SALAD, 46
GEORGIAN TOMATO AND CUCUMBER SALAD, 46
CHICKPEA AND KALE VEGETARIAN SOUP, 51
EGGPLANT AND CHICKPEA STEW, 54
STUFFED BELL PEPPERS, 58
VEGETABLE STUFFED ZUCCHINI BOATS, 60
SPICED LENTIL AND GROUND TURKEY SKILLET, 67

turkey breasts
BALSAMIC GLAZED TURKEY BREAST, 67

V

vegetable broth
MEDITERRANEAN LENTIL SOUP (VEGETARIAN), 49
SLOW-COOKED BEEF AND VEGETABLE SOUP, 51
CHICKPEA AND KALE VEGETARIAN SOUP, 51
HEARTY VEGETARIAN MINESTRONE SOUP, 52
QUINOA AND BLACK BEAN BOWL, 53
LENTIL AND SPINACH CURRY, 53
EGGPLANT AND CHICKPEA STEW, 54

MUSHROOM STROGANOFF, 59

W

walnuts
QUINOA BREAKFAST BOWL, 28
APPLE CINNAMON BAKED OATMEAL, 33
HOMEMADE GRANOLA WITH NUTS AND SEEDS, 34
GEORGIAN TOMATO AND CUCUMBER SALAD, 46
ARUGULA AND BEET SALAD, 48
DATE AND NUT ENERGY BITES, 78
FLAXSEED BREAD WITH WALNUTS AND RAISINS, 83
GEORGIAN EGGPLANT WITH WALNUTS, 46

whole grain bagels
SMOKED SALMON ON WHOLE GRAIN BAGEL WITH AVOCADO, 34

whole wheat breadcrumbs
SESAME GINGER TURKEY MEATBALLS, 64
HERB-CRUSTED BAKED COD, 70
MUSTARD AND HERB BAKED SALMON PATTIES, 71

whole wheat flour
PUMPKIN SPICE MUFFINS, 80
WHOLE GRAIN PANCAKES, 27
WHOLE-GRAIN FRUIT CRISP, 78
ZUCCHINI CHOCOLATE CAKE, 81

whole wheat tortillas
SPINACH AND FETA BREAKFAST WRAP (WHOLE WHEAT), 31

whole-grain bread
WHOLE GRAIN BREAD TOAST WITH GUACAMOLE, 25

whole-grain buns
VEGAN LENTIL SLOPPY JOES, 60

whole-grain crackers
TOMATO AND OLIVE TAPENADE ON CRACKERS, 38

whole-wheat pizza crust
WHOLE-WHEAT VEGGIE PIZZA, 56

wild rice
CHICKEN AND WILD RICE SOUP, 49

zucchini
TOFU SCRAMBLE WITH VEGETABLES, 32

BAKED MIXED VEGETABLE CHIPS, 36
SAUTÉED ZUCCHINI AND MUSHROOMS, 40
ZUCCHINI NOODLE SALAD, 42
ZUCCHINI SALAD WITH TAHINI DRESSING, 47
VEGETABLE STUFFED ZUCCHINI BOATS, 60
SLOW-COOKED MEDITERRANEAN CHICKEN STEW, 62
ZUCCHINI CHOCOLATE CAKE, 81
ZUCCHINI NOODLE ALFREDO, 56

Made in the USA
Las Vegas, NV
01 April 2025

20396468R10059